Football Supporters' Guide & Yearbook 2024

EDITOR

John Robinson

Thirtieth Edition

For details of our range of over 2,200 books and almost 200 DVDs, visit our web site or contact us using the information shown below.

British Library Cataloguing in Publication Data
A catalogue record for this book is available from the British Library

ISBN: 978-1-86223-503-8

72 St. Peter's Avenue, Cleethorpes, DN35 8HU, United Kingdom

Web site www.soccer-books.co.uk • e-mail info@soccer-books.co.uk

Printed in the UK by 4edge Ltd.

FOREWORD

Following a 3-year hiatus due to Covid-19 restrictions and other matters beyond our control, for this 30th Edition we have extended the 2022-2023 Statistical Results and Final Tables section to include all of the clubs in Steps 3 and 4 of the re-structured Non-League Football Pyramid.

Our thanks go to the numerous club officials who have aided us in the compilation of information contained in this guide as well as Michael Robinson (page layouts), Bob Budd (cover artwork) and Tony Brown (Cup Statistics – www.soccerdata.com).

Any readers who have up-to-date ground photographs which they would like us to consider for use in a future edition of this guide are requested to contact us at our address which is shown on the facing page.

We would like to wish our readers a safe and happy spectating season.

John Robinson
EDITOR

CONTENTS

The Vanarama National League

Address 4th Floor, 20 Waterloo Street, Birmingham B2 5TB

Web site www.thenationalleague.org.uk

Clubs for the 2023/2024 Season

AFC FYLDE

Photo courtesy of John Mills @ Altius Photography

Founded: 1988
Former Names: Formed by the amalgamation of Wesham FC and Kirkham Town FC in 1988
Nickname: 'The Coasters'
Ground: Mill Farm, Coronation Way, Wesham, Preston PR4 3JZ
Record Attendance: 3,858 (26th December 2016)

Colours: White shirts and shorts
Telephone Nº: (01772) 682593
Ground Capacity: 6,000
Seating Capacity: 2,000
Web Site: www.afcfylde.co.uk
E-mail: info@afcfylde.co.uk

GENERAL INFORMATION

Car Parking: A limited number of spaces are available at the ground (£5.00 charge) and there also is an overflow parking facility nearby.
Coach Parking: At the ground
Nearest Railway Station: Kirkham & Wesham (1 mile)
Club Shop: At the ground
Opening Times: Monday to Saturday 9.00am to 5.00pm. Tuesday Matchdays 10.00am to 10.00pm and Saturday Matchdays 9.00am to 6.00pm
Telephone Nº: (01772) 682593 (Phone orders accepted)

GROUND INFORMATION

Away Supporters' Entrances & Sections:
South Terrace standing and Seating in Block A.

ADMISSION INFO (2023/2024 PRICES)

Adult Standing: £12.00 – £16.00
Adult Seating: £20.00 – £35.00
Ages 12 to 17 Standing: £7.00
Ages 12 to 17 Seating: £8.00
Under-12s Seating: Free with an adult in North Stand

DISABLED INFORMATION

Wheelchairs: Accommodated
Helpers: Admitted
Prices: Normal prices apply for the disabled. One helper is admitted free of charge with each paying disabled fan.
Disabled Toilets: Available
Contact: (01772) 682593 (Bookings are necessary)

Travelling Supporters' Information:
Routes: The Mill Farm Sports Village is situated by the side of the A585, just to the north of Wesham and less than a mile to the south of Junction 3 of the M55.

ALDERSHOT TOWN FC

Founded: 2013 (as a new company)
Former Names: Aldershot Town FC
Nickname: 'Shots'
Ground: Ebb Stadium, High Street, Aldershot, GU11 1TW
Record Attendance: 7,500 (18th November 2000)
Colours: Red shirts with Blue Sleeves, Blue shorts

Telephone Nº: (01252) 320211
Ground Capacity: 7,100
Seating Capacity: 2,136
Web site: www.theshots.co.uk
E-mail: admin@theshots.co.uk

GENERAL INFORMATION

Car Parking: Parsons Barracks Car Park is adjacent
Coach Parking: Contact the club for information
Nearest Railway Station: Aldershot (5 mins. walk)
Nearest Bus Station: Aldershot (5 minutes walk)
Club Shop: At the ground
Opening Times: Weekdays 10.00am to 4.00pm, Saturday matchdays 10.00am to 2.45pm and 9.30am to 7.30pm on Tuesday matchdays. Times may be subject to change.
Telephone Nº: (01252) 320211

GROUND INFORMATION

Away Supporters' Entrances & Sections:
For unsegregated games, please use Turnstile 4 for accommodation in the Community Stand. For segregated games, accommodation will be in the South East Corner of the Stadium and The Bill Warren seats, in the South Stand.

ADMISSION INFO (2023/2024 PRICES)

Adult Standing/Seating: £20.00
Ages 11 to 18 Standing/Seating £7.00
Note: Under-11s are admitted free with paying adults buying Earlybird tickets.
Concessionary Standing/Seating: £16.00
Note: Military personnel are charged Concessionary prices and all Earlybird tickets are £2.00 cheaper than the above.

DISABLED INFORMATION

Wheelchairs: Accommodated in both the North Stand and the away section (Away fans use gate 45).
Helpers: Admitted
Prices: Concessionary prices for the disabled. Helpers free.
Disabled Toilets: Available
Contact: (01252) 320211 (Bookings are required)

Travelling Supporters' Information:
Routes: From the M3: Exit at Junction 4 and follow signs for Aldershot (A331). Leave the A331 at the A323 exit (Ash Road) and continue along into the High Street. The ground is just past the Railway Bridge on the right; From the A31: Continue along the A31 to the junction with the A331, then as above; From the A325 (Farnborough Road): Follow signs to the A323 then turn left into Wellington Avenue. The ground is just off the 2nd roundabout on the left – the floodlights are clearly visible.

ALTRINCHAM FC

Founded: 1891
Former Names: Broadheath FC
Nickname: 'The Robins'
Ground: The J. Davidson Stadium, Moss Lane, Altrincham WA15 8AP
Record Attendance: 10,275 (February 1925)
Colours: Red and White striped shirts, Black shorts
Telephone Nº: (0161) 928-1045
Ground Capacity: 6,085
Seating Capacity: 1,323
Web site: www.altrinchamfc.com
E-mail: office@altrinchamfootballclub.co.uk

GENERAL INFORMATION

Car Parking: Plenty of street parking is usually available in the proximity of the ground.
Coach Parking: By Police Direction
Nearest Railway Station: Altrincham (15 minutes walk)
Nearest Bus Station: Altrincham
Club Shop: Inside the ground
Opening Times: Weekdays 9.00am to 5.00pm
Telephone Nº: (0161) 928-1045

GROUND INFORMATION

Away Supporters' Entrances & Sections:
Hale End turnstiles and accommodation

ADMISSION INFO (2023/2024 PRICES)

Adult Standing/Seating: £20.00
Concessions (inc. NHS staff) Standing/Seating: £15.00
Juniors 12-18s Standing/Seating: £9.00
Children 5-11s Standing/Seating: £4.00 (£1.00 under-5s)

DISABLED INFORMATION

Wheelchairs: 3 spaces are available each for home and away fans adjacent to the Away dugout
Helpers: Admitted
Prices: Normal prices apply for disabled supporters. Helpers are admitted free of charge
Disabled Toilets: Yes
Contact: (0161) 928-1045 (Bookings are necessary)

Travelling Supporters' Information:
Routes: Exit the M56 at either Junction 6 or 7 and follow the signs for Altrincham FC.

BARNET FC

Founded: 1888
Former Names: Barnet Alston FC
Nickname: 'The Bees'
Ground: The Hive, Camrose Avenue, Edgware, HA8 6AG
Record Attendance: 6,215 (29th January 2019)

Colours: Shirts and shorts are Black and Amber
Telephone Nº: (020) 8381-3800
Ticket Office: (020) 8381-3800
Ground Capacity: 5,419 (All Seated)
Web site: www.barnetfc.com
E-mail: tellus@barnetfc.com

GENERAL INFORMATION

Car Parking: 350 spaces available at the ground
Coach Parking: Available at the ground
Nearest Railway Station: Harrow & Wealdstone (2½ miles)
Nearest Tube Station: Canons Park (5 minutes walk)
Club Shop: At the ground
Opening Times: Daily from 8.00am to 11.00pm – the shop is open throughout The Hive opening hours.
Telephone Nº: (020) 8381-3800

GROUND INFORMATION

Away Supporters' Entrances & Sections:
North Terrace and North West corner

ADMISSION INFO (2023/2024 PRICES)

Adult Seating: £22.00
Concessionary Seating: £14.00
Under-17s Seating: £5.00

FANS WITH DISABILITIES INFORMATION

Wheelchairs: 42 covered spaces in total for Home and Away fans in the East and West Stands
Helpers: One helper admitted per wheelchair
Prices: Normal prices for fans with disabilities. Helpers free
Disabled Toilets: Available
Contact: (020) 8381-3800 (Bookings are advisable)

Travelling Supporters' Information:
Routes: Exit the M1 at Junction 4 and take the Edgware Way/Watford Bypass (A41). Take the 3rd exit at the roundabout onto the A410 then the first exit at the next roundabout along the A5 (Stonegrove), continuing for approximately 1½ miles. Turn right into Camrose Avenue and The Hive is approximately two-thirds of a mile along this road.

BOREHAM WOOD FC

Founded: 1948
Former Names: Boreham Rovers FC and Royal Retournez FC
Nickname: 'The Wood'
Ground: Meadow Park, Broughinge Road, Borehamwood, Hertfordshire WD6 5AL
Record Attendance: 4,030 (2001 vs Arsenal)

Colours: White shirts and shorts
Telephone N°: (0208) 953-5097
Ground Capacity: 4,500
Seating Capacity: 1,700
Web site: www.borehamwoodfootballclub.co.uk

GENERAL INFORMATION

Car Parking: Brook Road car park is nearby
Coach Parking: Please contact the club for details
Nearest Railway Station: Elstree & Borehamwood (1 mile)
Nearest Bus Station: Barnet
Club Shop: At the ground
Opening Times: 9.00am to 10.00pm Monday to Thursday; 9.00am to 6.00pm at weekends
Telephone N°: (0208) 953-5097

GROUND INFORMATION

Away Supporters' Entrances & Sections:
Use the Away Gate in the West Stand for access to South Stand accommodation.

ADMISSION INFO (2023/2024 PRICES)

Adult Standing/Seating: £20.00
Under-16s Standing/Seating: £12.00
Under-12s Standing/Seating: £6.00
Senior Citizen Standing/Seating: £18.00
Note:: Tickets are cheaper for Black Card members.

DISABLED INFORMATION

Wheelchairs: Accommodated in the West Stand
Helpers: Admitted
Prices: Normal prices are charged for the disabled. Helpers are admitted free of charge.
Disabled Toilets: Available
Contact: (0208) 953-5097 (Bookings are not necessary)

Travelling Supporters' Information:
Routes: Exit the M25 at Junction 23 and take the A1 South. After 2 miles, take the Borehamwood exit onto the dual carriageway and go over the flyover following signs for Borehamwood for 1 mile. Turn right at the Studio roundabout into Brook Road, then next right into Broughinge Road for the ground.

BROMLEY FC

Founded: 1892
Former Names: None
Nickname: 'The Ravens'
Ground: The Stadium, Hayes Lane, Bromley, Kent, BR2 9EF
Record Attendance: 10,798 (24th September 1949)

Colours: White shirts with Black shorts
Telephone Nº: (020) 8460-5291
Ground Capacity: 5,000
Seating Capacity: 1,300
Web site: www.bromleyfc.co.uk
E-mail: info@bromleyfc.co.uk

GENERAL INFORMATION

Car Parking: 300 spaces available at the ground
Coach Parking: At the ground
Nearest Railway Station: Bromley South (1 mile)
Nearest Bus Station: High Street, Bromley
Club Shop: At the ground
Opening Times: Matchdays only
Telephone Nº: (020) 8460-5291

GROUND INFORMATION

Away Supporters' Entrances & Sections:
No usual segregation

ADMISSION INFO (2023/2024 PRICES)

Adult Standing/Seating: £20.00 (£22.00)
Concessionary Standing/Seating: £15.00 (£17.00)
Under-16s/Student Standing/Seating: £7.00 (£9.00)
Note: Prices shown are for tickets purchased in advance. Tickets purchased just before the game are more expensive (prices shown above in brackets). Discounted prices are available on the matchday for online bookings before 1.30pm or 6.30pm for day and night matches respectively. Under-11s are admitted free of charge with a paying adult for advance purchases up to 1 hour before kick-off.

DISABLED INFORMATION

Wheelchairs: Accommodated
Prices: Concessionary prices are charged for disabled fans. Helpers are admitted free of charge
Disabled Toilets: Available
Contact: (0181) 460-5291 (Bookings are necessary) – David Cook (Disability Liaison Officer) – 07786 068569

Travelling Supporters' Information:
Routes: Exit the M25 at Junction 4 and follow the A21 for Bromley and London for approximately 4 miles before forking left onto the A232 signposted for Croydon/Sutton. At the second set of traffic lights turn right into Baston Road (B265) and follow for approximately 2 miles as it becomes Hayes Street and then Hayes Lane. The ground is on the right just after a mini-roundabout.

CHESTERFIELD FC

Founded: 1866
Former Names: Chesterfield Municipal FC, Chesterfield Town FC
Nickname: 'Spireites' 'Blues'
Ground: SMH Group Stadium , 1866 Sheffield Road, Whittington Moor, Chesterfield S41 8NZ
Ground Capacity: 10,000 (All seats)

Record Attendance: 30,968 (Saltergate – 7/4/1939)
Colours: Blue shirts with White shorts
Telephone Nº: (01246) 269300
Ticket Office: (01246) 269300 (Option 1)
Web Site: www.chesterfield-fc.co.uk

GENERAL INFORMATION

Car Parking: Various Car Parks available nearby
Coach Parking: At the ground
Nearest Railway Station: Chesterfield (1¼ miles)
Nearest Bus Station: Chesterfield
Club Shop: At the ground
Opening Times: Please contact the club for details
Telephone Nº: (01246) 209765

GROUND INFORMATION

Away Supporters' Entrances & Sections:
H. Lilleker North Stand Turnstiles

ADMISSION INFO (2023/2024 PRICES)

Adult Seating: £20.00 – £24.00
Ages 17 to 21 Seating: £17.00 – £21.00
Juvenile (Under-17s) Seating: £9.00
Concessionary Seating: £17.00 – £21.00
Under-7s Seating: £7.00 in the Family Stand

FANS WITH DISABILITIES INFORMATION

Wheelchairs: Up to 96 spaces available around the ground
Note: Lifts are available in the East and West stands
Helpers: One helper admitted per fan with disabilities
Prices: Normal prices for disabled fans. Free for helpers.
Disabled Toilets: Available in all stands
Contact: (01246) 269300 (Bookings are advised)
Peter Whiteley (Disability Liaison Officer) –
peterwhiteley@chesterfield-fc.co.uk

Travelling Supporters' Information:
Routes: From the South: Exit the M1 at Junction 29 and follow the A617 for Chesterfield. At the roundabout, take the 4th exit and head north on the A61 Sheffield Road and the stadium is located in the Whittington Moor district next to the junction with the A619; From the East: Take the A619 to Chesterfield and the ground is situated next to the Tesco supermarket at the junction with the A61; From the North: Exit the M1 at Junction 30 and take the A619 to Chesterfield. Then as above.

DAGENHAM & REDBRIDGE FC

Founded: 1992 (**Entered League**: 2007)
Former Names: Formed by the merger of Dagenham FC and Redbridge Forest FC
Nickname: 'The Daggers'
Ground: Chigwell Construction Stadium, Victoria Road, Dagenham RM10 7XL
Record Attendance: 5,949 (vs Ipswich Town in 2002)

Colours: Red shirts with Blue shorts
Telephone Nº: (020) 8592-1549
Ground Capacity: 6,078
Seating Capacity: 2,233
Web site: www.daggers.co.uk
E-mail: info@daggers.co.uk

GENERAL INFORMATION

Car Parking: Street parking only
Coach Parking: Street parking only
Nearest Railway Station: Dagenham East (5 mins. walk)
Nearest Bus Station: Romford
Club Shop: At the ground
Opening Times: Monday & Tuesday 12.00pm – 4.00pm; Thursday 12.00pm – 8.00pm; Friday 12.00pm – 6.00pm; Saturday matchdays 1.00pm – 3.00pm.
Closed on Wednesdays, Sundays and non-match Saturdays
Telephone Nº: (020) 8592-7194

GROUND INFORMATION

Away Supporters' Entrances & Sections:
Pondfield Road entrances for West Stand accommodation

ADMISSION INFO (2023/2024 PRICES)

Adult Standing: £19.00
Adult Seating: £19.00 – £25.00
Concessionary Standing: £14.00
Concessionary Seating: £14.00 – £19.00
Under-16s Standing: £10.00 (Under-10s free of charge)
Under-16s Seating: £10.00 – £14.00
Under-10s Seating: £2.00 (Free in the Family Stand)
(Tickets booked in advance are £2.00 less)

DISABLED INFORMATION

Wheelchairs: Accommodated in front of the new Stand and the Family Stand
Helpers: Admitted
Prices: £19.00 for the disabled. Free of charge for Helpers
Disabled Toilets: Available at the East and West ends of the ground and also in the Clubhouse
Contact: (020) 8592-7194 Ext. 4 (Bookings are necessary)
Charlie Fraser (Club Secretary) – secretary@daggers.cc.uk

Travelling Supporters' Information:
Routes: From the North & West: Take the M11 to its end and join the A406 South. At the large roundabout take the slip road on the left signposted A13 to Dagenham. As you approach Dagenham, stay in the left lane and follow signs for A1306 signposted Dagenham East. Turn left onto the A1112 at the 5th set of traffic lights by the McDonalds. Proceed along Ballards Road to The Bull roundabout and bear left. Victoria Road is 450 yards on the left after passing Dagenham East tube station; From the South & East: Follow signs for the A13 to Dagenham. Take the next slip road off signposted Elm Park & Dagenham East then turn right at the roundabout. Go straight on at the next roundabout and turn left onto A1306. After ½ mile you will see a McDonalds on the right. Get into the right hand filter lane and turn right onto A1112. Then as from the North & West. **SatNav**: RM10 7XL

DORKING WANDERERS FC

Photo courtesy of John Mills @ Altius Photography

Founded: 1999
Former Names: None
Nickname: 'Wanderers'
Ground: Meadowbank Stadium, Mill Lane, Dorking, RH4 1DX
Record Attendance: 1,604 (January 2020 vs Stockport County)
Colours: Red and White striped shirts with Blue shorts
Telephone Nº: (01306) 400151
Ground Capacity: 3,000
Seating Capacity: 522
Web site: www.dorkingwanderers.com
E-mail: info@dorkingwanderers.com

GENERAL INFORMATION

Car Parking: Limited number of spaces at the ground. St. Martins Walk car park is 2 minutes walk from the stadium.
Coach Parking: Please contact the club for information.
Nearest Railway Station: Dorking West (½ mile)
Nearest Bus Station: Nearest bus stop is at The White Hart (Stop K)
Club Shop: At the ground
Opening Times: Matchdays only plus online sales
Telephone Nº: (01306) 400151

GROUND INFORMATION

Away Supporters' Entrances & Sections:
No usual segregation

ADMISSION INFO (2023/2024 PRICES)

Adult Standing/Seating: £18.00
Concessionary Standing/Seating: £16.00
Under-18s Standing/Seating: £9.00
Under-8s Standing/Seating: £5.00

DISABLED INFORMATION

Wheelchairs: Accommodated
Helpers: Admitted
Prices: Please contact the club for details
Disabled Toilets: Available
Contact: (01306) 400151 (Bookings are necessary)

Travelling Supporters' Information:
Routes: From the North: Exit the M25 at Junction 9 and follow the A24 southwards to Dorking. Upon reaching Dorking, take the 3rd exit at the Deepdene Roundabout onto the A25 (Reigate Road) and continue into the High Street. Turn right into Mill Lane by The White Horse pub for the ground; From the South: Follow the A24 northwards to Dorking. Take the first exit at the Deepdene Roundabout onto Reigate Road, then as above; From the West: Follow the A25 eastwards to Dorking, continue into the High Street, then turn right by The White Horse pub into Mill Lane for the ground; From the East: Follow the A25 westward into Dorking, continue into the High Street, then turn left into Mill Lane for the ground.

EASTLEIGH FC

Founded: 1946
Former Names: Swaythling Athletic FC and Swaythling FC
Nickname: 'The Spitfires'
Ground: The Silverlake Stadium, Stoneham Lane, Eastleigh SO50 9HT
Record Attendance: 5,025 (2016 vs Bolton Wands.)

Colours: Blue shirts, shorts and socks
Telephone Nº: (023) 8061-3361
Fax Number: (023) 8061-2379
Ground Capacity: 5,192
Seating Capacity: 3,210
Web site: www.eastleighfc.com
e-mail: admin@eastleighfc.com

GENERAL INFORMATION

Car Parking: Spaces for 450 cars (hard standing – £5.00)
Coach Parking: At the ground
Nearest Railway Station: Southampton Parkway (¾ mile)
Nearest Bus Station: Eastleigh (2 miles)
Club Shop: At the ground
Opening Times: Monday to Friday 10.00am to 4.00pm plus Saturday and Weekdays Matchdays 9.00am until kick-off, then for 30 minutes after the game.
Telephone Nº: (023) 8061-3361

GROUND INFORMATION

Away Supporters' Entrances & Sections:
Mackoy Community Stand, Blocks 1, 2 & 3 – entrance via Turnstiles 10 and 11

ADMISSION INFO (2023/2024 PRICES)

Adult Standing: £20.00 **Adult Seating**: £21.00 – £22.50
Concessionary Standing: £15.00
Concessionary Seating: £16.00-£17.50
Juniors 7-16s Standing/Seating: £7.00 – £9.50
Under-7s Standing/Seating: £5.00 – £7.50
Note: Discounted prices are available for advance purchases

DISABLED INFORMATION

Wheelchairs: 24 spaces for home fans in the Mackoy (South) Stand plus 2 in the West Stand. A further 7 spaces are available in the Mackoy Stand for away fans.
Helpers: Admitted
Prices: Normal prices for the disabled. Helpers free of charge
Disabled Toilets: Available in Nuffield Health Stand
Contact: (023) 8061-3361 (Bookings are not necessary) – Sarah Woolley – dlo@eastleighfc.com

Travelling Supporters' Information:
Routes: Exit the M27 at Junction 5 (signposted for Southampton Airport) and take the A335 (Stoneham Way) towards Southampton. After ½ mile, turn right at the traffic lights into Bassett Green Road. Turn right at the next set of traffic lights into Stoneham Lane and the ground is on the right after ¾ mile.

EBBSFLEET UNITED FC

Founded: 1946
Former Names: Gravesend & Northfleet United FC, Gravesend United FC and Northfleet United FC
Nickname: 'The Fleet'
Ground: The Kuflink Stadium, Stonebridge Road, Northfleet, Gravesend, Kent DA11 9GN
Record Attendance: 12,036 (vs Sunderland 1963)

Colours: Reds shirts and shorts
Telephone Nº: (01474) 533796
Ground Capacity: 4,769
Seating Capacity: 2,179
Web site: www.ebbsfleetunited.co.uk
E-mail: info@eufc.co.uk

GENERAL INFORMATION

Car Parking: Ebbsfleet International Car Park C (when available) and also street parking
Coach Parking: At the ground
Nearest Railway Station: Northfleet (5 minutes walk)
Nearest Bus Station: Bus Stop outside the ground
Club Shop: At the ground plus online sales
Opening Times: Weekdays 9.00am to 5.00pm
Telephone Nº: (01474) 533796

GROUND INFORMATION

Away Supporters' Entrances & Sections:
Only certain games are segregated, when the Swanscombe End turnstiles are allocated to away supporters.
Please contact the club for further details

ADMISSION INFO (2023/2024 PRICES)

Adult Standing: £15.00
Adult Seating: £15.00
Concessionary Standing/Seating: £12.00
Under-17s Standing/Seating: £7.00
Under-12s Standing/Seating: £1.00 when accompanied by a paying adult (maximum of 2 per adult).

DISABLED INFORMATION

Wheelchairs: 6 spaces are available in the Disabled Area in front of the Main Stand
Helpers: Admitted free of charge
Prices: Normal prices apply for disabled fans
Disabled Toilets: Available in the Main Stand
Contact: (01474) 533796 (Bookings are necessary)

Travelling Supporters' Information:
Routes: Take the A2 to the Northfleet/Southfleet exit and follow signs for Northfleet (B262). Go straight on at the first roundabout then take the 2nd exit at the 2nd roundabout into Thames Way and follow the football signs for the ground.

FC HALIFAX TOWN

Founded: 1911 (Re-formed 2008)
Former Names: Halifax Town FC
Nickname: 'The Shaymen'
Ground: The Shay Stadium, Shay Syke, Halifax, HX1 2YT
Ground Capacity: 10,568
Seating Capacity: 5,285

Record Attendance: 8,042 (vs Bradford City, 2014)
Colours: Blue shirts and shorts
Telephone N°: (01422) 341222
Web Site: www.fchalifaxtown.co.uk
E-mail: tonyallan@fchalifaxtown.co.uk

GENERAL INFORMATION

Car Parking: Adjacent to the East Stand and also Shaw Hill Car Park (Nearby)
Coach Parking: By arrangement with the Club Secretary
Nearest Railway Station: Halifax (10 minutes walk)
Nearest Bus Station: Halifax (15 minutes walk)
Club Shop: At the ground in the East Stand
Opening Times: Please phone for details
Telephone N°: (01422) 341222

GROUND INFORMATION

Away Supporters' Entrances & Sections:
Skircoat Stand (Seating only)

ADMISSION INFO (2023/2024 PRICES)

Adult Standing/Seating: £21.00
Senior Citizen Standing/Seating: £18.00
Under-18s Standing/Seating: £9.00
Under-12s Standing/Seating: £4.00

DISABLED INFORMATION

Wheelchairs: 33 spaces available in total in disabled sections in the East Stand on the 2nd & 3rd tier levels
Helpers: One admitted free with each paying disabled fan
Prices: Free of charge for the disabled and helpers
Disabled Toilets: Available in the East Stand, both levels
Contact: (01422) 886802 (Bookings are not necessary)

Travelling Supporters' Information:
Routes: From the North: Take the A629 to Halifax Town Centre. Take the 2nd exit at the roundabout into Broad Street and follow signs for Huddersfield (A629) into Skircoat Road; From the South, East and West: Exit the M62 at Junction 24 and follow Halifax (A629) signs for the Town Centre into Skircoat Road then Shaw Hill for ground. **SatNav**: Use HX1 2YS for the ground.

GATESHEAD FC

Founded: 1930 (Reformed in 1977)
Former Names: Gateshead United FC
Nickname: 'Tynesiders'
Ground: International Stadium, Neilson Road, Gateshead NE10 0EF
Record Attendance: 11,750 (vs Newcastle Utd, 1995)
Colours: White shirts with Black shorts
Telephone Nº: (0191) 477-1983
Ground Capacity: 11,750 (All seats)
Web site: www.gateshead-fc.com
E-mail: info@gateshead-fc.com

GENERAL INFORMATION

Car Parking: At the stadium
Coach Parking: At the stadium
Nearest Railway Station: Gateshead Stadium Metro (½ mile); Newcastle (British Rail) 1½ miles
Nearest Bus Station: Newcastle Coach Station, St. James' Boulevard, Newcastle-upon-Tyne, NE1 4BW (2½ miles)
Club Shop: At the stadium
Opening Times: Matchdays only
Telephone Nº: (0191) 477-1983

GROUND INFORMATION

Away Supporters' Entrances & Sections:
East Stand

ADMISSION INFO (2023/2024 PRICES)

Adult Seating: £15.00
Senior Citizen/Concessionary Seating: £10.00
Under-18s/Student Seating: £5.00

DISABLED INFORMATION

Wheelchairs: 5 spaces available each for home and away fans on the balcony (covered area)
Helpers: Admitted
Prices: Normal prices for the disabled. Helpers are admitted free of charge.
Disabled Toilets: Available in the Reception Area and on the 1st floor concourse – accessible by lift.
Contact: (0191) 477-1983 (Bookings are necessary)

Travelling Supporters' Information:
Routes: From the South: Take the A1(M) to Washington Services and fork right onto the A194(M) signposted Tyne Tunnel. At the next roundabout, turn left onto the A184 signposted for Gateshead. The Stadium is on the right after 3 miles.

HARTLEPOOL UNITED FC

Founded: 1908
Former Names: Hartlepools United FC (1908-68); Hartlepool FC (1968-77)
Nickname: 'The Pool' 'Pools'
Ground: Victoria Park, Clarence Road, Hartlepool TS24 8BZ
Ground Capacity: 7,865 **Seating Capacity**: 4,359
Record Attendance: 17,426 (15th January 1957)

Colours: Blue and White striped shirts with Blue shorts
Telephone Nº: (01429) 272584
Ticket Office: (01429) 272584 Option 2
Ticket Office e-mail: tickets@hartlepoolunited.co.uk
Web Site: www.hartlepoolunited.co.uk
E-mail: enquiries@hartlepoolunited.co.uk

GENERAL INFORMATION

Car Parking: Limited space at the ground (£5.00 charge) and also street parking
Coach Parking: Church Street
Nearest Railway Station: Hartlepool Church Street (5 minutes walk)
Club Shop: At the ground
Opening Times: Monday to Friday 10.00am to 4.00pm and Saturday Matchdays 10.00am to 3.00pm.
Telephone Nº: (01429) 272584

GROUND INFORMATION

Away Supporters' Entrances & Sections:
Clarence Road turnstiles 1 & 2 for Smith & Graham Stand

ADMISSION INFO (2023/2024 PRICES)

Adult Standing/Seating: £20.00 (£21.00 on the day)
Concessions Standing/Seating: £14.00 (£15.00 on day)
Under-14s: Admitted for £5.00 with a paying adult
Under-5s: Free with a paying adult

DISABLED INFORMATION

Wheelchairs: 14 spaces for Home fans in disabled section, Camerons CK Stand, 10 spaces for Away fans in the Smith & Graham Stand.
Helpers: One helper admitted per wheelchair
Prices: Normal prices for disabled fans. Helpers free of charge
Disabled Toilets: Available around the ground
Contact: (01429) 272584 Option 9 (Bookings advisable): Neil Appleyard (0774 7735247) neilappleyard@hotmail.com

Travelling Supporters' Information: **Routes**: From the North: Take the A1/A19 to the A179 and follow Town Centre/ Marina signs. Turn right at the roundabout by the 'Historic Quayside' and cross over the Railway bridge. The ground is on the left; From the South & West: Take the A689 following Town Centre/Marina signs. Turn left at the roundabout by the 'Historic Quayside' and cross over the Railway bridge. The ground is on the left.

KIDDERMINSTER HARRIERS FC

Founded: 1886
Nickname: 'Harriers'
Ground: Aggborough Stadium, Hoo Road, Kidderminster DY10 1NB
Ground Capacity: 6,444
Seating Capacity: 3,140
Record Attendance: 9,155 (vs Hereford, 1948)

Colours: Red shirts with White sleeves, Red shorts
Telephone Nº: (01562) 823931
Web Site: www.harriers.co.uk
E-mail: info@harriers.co.uk

GENERAL INFORMATION

Car Parking: At the ground (£3.00 to £5.00 per car)
Coach Parking: As directed
Nearest Railway Station: Kidderminster
Nearest Bus Station: Kidderminster Town Centre
Club Shop: At the ground
Opening Times: Weekdays 9.00am to 5.00pm. Saturday matchdays 11.00am to 3.00pm then 4.45pm to 5.30pm and midweek matchdays 9.00am to 8.00pm then for an hour after the game.
Telephone Nº: (01562) 823931

GROUND INFORMATION

Away Supporters' Entrances & Sections:
East Stand for seating and South Stand Terrace for standing

ADMISSION INFO (2023/2024 PRICES)

Adult Standing: £18.00
Adult Seating: £20.00
Concessionary Standing: £14.00
Concessionary Seating: £16.00
Students 16-21 Standing/Seating: £12.00 – £14.00
Under-16s Standing/Seating: £5.00 – £6.00

DISABLED INFORMATION

Wheelchairs: Home fans accommodated at the front of the Main Stand, Away fans in front of the East Stand
Helpers: Admitted
Prices: Normal prices for disabled fans. Helpers are admitted free of charge.
Disabled Toilets: Available by the disabled area
Contact: (01562) 823931 (Bookings are not necessary)

Travelling Supporters' Information:
Routes: Exit the M5 at Junction 3 and follow the A456 to Kidderminster. The ground is situated close by the Severn Valley Railway Station so follow the brown Steam Train signs and turn into Hoo Road about 200 yards downhill of the station. Follow the road along for ¼ mile and the ground is on the left.

MAIDENHEAD UNITED FC

Founded: 1870
Former Names: None
Nickname: 'Magpies'
Ground: York Road, Maidenhead, Berks. SL6 1SF
Ground Capacity: 4,000
Seating Capacity: 550

Record Attendance: 7,920 (vs Southall in 1936)
Colours: Black and White striped shirts, Black shorts
Telephone Nº: (01628) 636314 (Club)
Web: www.maidenheadunitedfc.org
E-mail: social@maidenheadunitedfc.org

GENERAL INFORMATION

Car Parking: Grove Road and Town Hall car parks
Coach Parking: Grove Road and Town Hall car parks
Nearest Railway Station: Maidenhead (¼ mile)
Nearest Bus Station: Maidenhead
Club Shop: At the ground
Opening Times: Matchdays only
Telephone Nº: (01628) 624739

GROUND INFORMATION

Away Supporters' Entrances & Sections:
No usual segregation

ADMISSION INFO (2023/2024 PRICES)

Adult Standing: £20.00
Adult Seating: £20.00
Concessionary Standing/Seating: £15.00
Next Generation (17-22yrs)Standing/Seating: £10.00
Under-17s Standing and Seating: £5.00

DISABLED INFORMATION

Wheelchairs: Accommodated
Helpers: Admitted
Prices: Normal prices for the disabled. Free for helpers
Disabled Toilets: Available
Contact: (01628) 636314 (Bookings are not necessary)

Travelling Supporters' Information:
Routes: Exit M4 at Junction 7 and take the A4 to Maidenhead. Cross the River Thames bridge and turn left at the 2nd roundabout passing through the traffic lights. York Road is first right and the ground is approximately 300 yards along on the left.

OLDHAM ATHLETIC FC

Founded: 1895 (**Entered League**: 1907)
Former Names: Pine Villa FC (1895-1899)
Nickname: 'Latics'
Ground: Boundary Park, Furtherwood Road, Oldham OL1 2PA
Ground Capacity: 13,513 (All seats)
Record Attendance: 47,671 (25th January 1930)

Colours: Blue shirts, shorts and socks
Telephone N°: (0161) 624-4972
Ticket Office: (0161) 785-5150
Web Site: www.oldhamathletic.co.uk
E-mail: enquiries@oldhamathletic.co.uk

GENERAL INFORMATION

Car Parking: 350 spaces in North Stand car park (permit holders only) and also the nearby Hospital car park (£5.00)
Coach Parking: At the ground
Nearest Railway Station: Oldham Werneth (1½ miles)
Nearest Bus Station: Oldham Town Centre (2 miles)
Club Shop: In the North Stand
Opening Times: Tuesday to Saturday 10.00am to 3.00pm.
Telephone N°: (0161) 624-4972

GROUND INFORMATION

Away Supporters' Entrances & Sections:
Chadderton Road Stand

ADMISSION INFO (2023/2024 PRICES)

Adult Seating: £24.00
Concessionary Seating: £12.00
Under-18s Seating: £10.00
Under-12s Seating: £3.00 (with a paying adult)
Note: Discounts are available for tickets purchased in advance.

FANS WITH DISABILITIES INFORMATION

Wheelchairs: 60 spaces in the special areas in the North Stand, Chadderton Road Stand and Rochdale Road Stand
Helpers: One helper admitted per fan with disabilities if on the higher/enhanced rate of care
Prices: Normal prices for fans with disabilities. Helpers free
Disabled Toilets: Available in the North Stand, Rochdale Road Stand and the Chadderton Road Stand
Contact: (0161) 785-5179 (Bookings are necessary)
Pamela Makin (Disability Liaison Officer) on 0161-6244972

Travelling Supporters' Information:
Routes: From All Parts: Exit the M62 at Junction 20 and take the A627M to the junction with the A664. Take the 1st exit at the roundabout onto Broadway, then the 1st right into Hilbre Avenue which leads to the car park at the ground.

OXFORD CITY FC

Founded: 1882
Former Names: None
Nickname: 'City'
Ground: RAW Charging Stadium, Marsh Lane, Marston, Oxford OX3 0NQ
Record Attendance: 9,500 (vs Leytonstone, 1950)

Colours: Blue & White hooped shirts with Blue shorts
Telephone Nº: (01865) 744493
Ground Capacity: 3,218
Seating Capacity: 520
Web Site: www.oxfordcityfc.co.uk
E-mail: club@oxcityfc.co.uk

GENERAL INFORMATION

Car Parking: At the ground
Coach Parking: At the ground
Nearest Railway Station: Oxford (3¾ miles)
Club Shop: At the ground
Opening Times: Matchdays only
Telephone Nº: (01865) 744493

GROUND INFORMATION

Away Supporters' Entrances & Sections:
No usual segregation

ADMISSION INFO (2023/2024 PRICES)

Adult Standing: £13.00
Adult Seating: £13.00
Concessionary/Student Standing: £8.00
Concessionary/Student Seating: £8.00
Under-18s Standing: Free if tickets bought in advance
Under-18s Seating: Free if tickets bought in advance
Note: All ticket prices shown above are £2.00 more on Matchdays

DISABLED INFORMATION

Wheelchairs: Accommodated
Helpers: Admitted
Prices: Normal prices apply for the disabled and helpers
Disabled Toilets: Available
Contact: (01865) 744493 (Bookings are not necessary)

Travelling Supporters' Information:
Routes: The stadium is located by the side of the A40 Northern Bypass Road next to the Marston flyover junction to the north east of Oxford. Exit the A40 at the Marston junction and head into Marsh Lane (B4150). Take the first turn on the left into the OXSRAD Complex then turn immediately left again to follow the approach road to the stadium in the far corner of the site.

ROCHDALE AFC

Founded: 1907 (**Entered League**: 1921)
Former Names: Rochdale Town FC
Nickname: 'The Dale'
Ground: The Crown Oil Arena, Rochdale OL11 5DR
Ground Capacity: 10,249
Seating Capacity: 7,913
Record Attendance: 24,231 (10th December 1949)

Colours: Blue and Black striped shirts with Blue shorts
Telephone Nº: (01706) 644648
Ticket Office: (01706) 644648 Option 8
Web Site: www.rochdaleafc.co.uk
E-mail: office@rochdaleafc.co.uk

GENERAL INFORMATION

Car Parking: Street parking only
Coach Parking: By Police direction
Nearest Railway Station: Rochdale (2 miles)
Nearest Bus Station: Town Centre (1 mile)
Club Shop: At the ground
Opening Times: Weekdays 9.00am to 5.00pm, Saturday matchdays from 9.00am to 3.00pm then open again after the final whistle. Other Saturdays from 9.00am to 12.00pm
Telephone Nº: (01706) 644648 Option 3

GROUND INFORMATION

Away Supporters' Entrances & Sections:
Turnstiles 11 to 18 for Willbutts Lane

ADMISSION INFO (2023/2024 PRICES)

Adult Standing: £20.00
Adult Seating: £22.00 – £24.00
Senior Citizen Standing/Seating: £17.00 – £19.00
Ages 16 to 21 Standing/Seating: £10.00 – £14.00
Juniors under-14 Standing/Seating: £5.00 – £7.00
Note: Certain tickets are cheaper if purchased in advance and under 14s must be with a paying adult.

FANS WITH DISABILITIES INFORMATION

Wheelchairs: 33 spaces in total in special sections in the Main, Pearl Street and Willbutts Lane Stands
Helpers: One helper admitted per fan with disabilities
Prices: Concessionary prices are charged for wheelchair users. Ambulant fans with disabilities pay normal prices. Helpers are admitted free of charge
Disabled Toilets: Available
Contact: Nicola Toolan (Disability Liaison Officer) – 07706 753594 – nicola.toolan@rochdaleafc.co.uk

Travelling Supporters' Information:
Routes: From All Parts: Exit the M62 at Junction 20 and take the A627(M) signposted Rochdale. At the end of this link road, filter left carry on for 400 yards and go straight on at the roundabout into Roche Valley Way signposted Spotland Stadium. At the traffic lights go staight ahead and the ground is on the right after ½ mile.

SOUTHEND UNITED FC

Founded: 1906 (**Entered League**: 1920)
Former Name: Southend Athletic FC
Nickname: 'Shrimpers' 'Blues'
Ground: Roots Hall Ground, Victoria Avenue, Southend-on-Sea SS2 6NQ
Ground Capacity: 12,392 (All seats)
Record Attendance: 31,033 (10th January 1979)

Colours: Blue shirts and shorts
Telephone N°: (01702) 304050
Web Site: www.southendunited.co.uk
E-mail: info@southend-united.co.uk

GENERAL INFORMATION

Car Parking: Available at Southend High School for Boys (Post code SS0 0RG). £5.00 fee and a 10 minute walk
Coach Parking: Car park at the ground. Coach drivers should contact the club prior to the game
Nearest Railway Station: Prittlewell (¼ mile)
Nearest Bus Station: London Road, Southend
Club Shop: At the ground
Opening Times: Monday to Friday 9.30am to 5.00pm and Saturday Matchdays 10.00am to 3.00pm
Telephone N°: (01702) 351117

GROUND INFORMATION

Away Supporters' Entrances & Sections:
Turnstiles 13 to 16 for North Stand seating

ADMISSION INFO (2023/2024 PRICES)

Adult Seating: £20.00
Concessionary Seating: £15.00
Under-23s/Student Seating: £15.00
Under-17s Seating: £10.00
Under-9s Seating: £5.00
Note: Tickets are cheaper when purchased in advance.

FANS WITH DISABILITIES INFORMATION

Wheelchairs: 20 spaces for Home fans and and 6 spaces for Away fans in a special section in the West Stand
Helpers: One helper admitted per fan with disabilities
Prices: Concessionary prices apply for fans with disabilities. Helpers receive complimentary tickets
Disabled Toilets: Available – Radar key required
Commentaries are available for the blind
Contact: (01702) 304050 (Gavin Preston)
or e-mail ticket.officemanager@southend-united.co.uk

Travelling Supporters' Information:
Routes: From the North and West: From the M25 take Junction 29 and follow the A127 to Southend. About 1 mile outside of Southend Town Centre, take the 3rd exit at the roundabout into Victoria Avenue for the ground; From the A13: Follow signs for Southend, turn left into West Road at Westcliff. At the end of West Road turn left into Victoria Avenue – the ground is on the left.

SOLIHULL MOORS FC

Photo courtesy of Jordan Martin Photography

Founded: 2007
Former Names: Formed by the merger of Solihull Borough FC and Moor Green FC in 2007
Nickname: 'The Moors'
Ground: The Armco Arena, Damson Parkway, Solihull B92 9EJ
Record Attendance: 3,681 (vs AFC Fylde, 2019)
Colours: Yellow and Blue shirts with Blue shorts
Telephone Nº: (0121) 705-6770
Ground Capacity: 4,510
Seating Capacity: 2,522
Web site: www.solihullmoorsfc.co.uk
E-mail: info@solihullmoorsfc.co.uk

GENERAL INFORMATION

Car Parking: Limited number of spaces at the ground (£5.00 charge per car)
Coach Parking: At the ground
Nearest Railway Station: Birmingham International (2 miles)
Nearest Bus Station: Birmingham (5 miles)
Club Shop: At the ground
Opening Times: Monday to Friday and Saturday Matchdays 10.00am to 4.00pm (but closed on Wednesdays)
Telephone Nº: (0121) 705-6770

GROUND INFORMATION

Away Supporters' Entrances & Sections:
No usual segregation

ADMISSION INFO (2023/2024 PRICES)

Adult Standing/Seating: £16.00 – £21.00
Senior Citizen/18s to 24s Standing: £12.00
Senior Citizen/18s to 24s Seating: £16.00
Ages 12-18 Standing/Seating: £7.50
Under 12s Standing/Seating: £3.50
Note: Under-12s must be accompanied by a paying Adult or Concession

DISABLED INFORMATION

Wheelchairs: 10 spaces in the Damson Homes Stand
Helpers: Admitted
Prices: Normal prices for fans with disabilities. Helpers free
Disabled Toilets: Available in the Damson Homes Stand
Contact: (0121) 705-6770 (Becci Fox)

Travelling Supporters' Information:
Routes: Exit the M42 at Junction 6 and take the A45 for 2 miles towards Birmingham. Turn left at the traffic lights near the Posthouse Hotel into Damson Parkway (signposted for Landrover/Damsonwood). Continue to the roundabout and come back along the other carriageway to the ground which is situated on the left after about 150 yards.

WEALDSTONE FC

Founded: 1899
Former Names: None
Nickname: 'The Stones' or 'The Royals'
Ground: Grosvenor Vale, Ruislip HA4 6JQ
Ground Capacity: 3,607
Seating Capacity: 709
Record Attendance: 2,469 (vs Colchester Utd, 2015)

Colours: Royal Blue shirts with White shorts
Contact Telephone Nº: 07790 038095 (Paul Fruin – Club Secretary)
Web site: www.wealdstone-fc.com
E-mail: wealdstonefc@btinternet.com

GENERAL INFORMATION

Car Parking: 100 spaces available at the ground
Coach Parking: Available outside the ground
Nearest Mainline Station: West Ruislip (1 mile)
Nearest Tube Station: Ruislip (½ mile)
Club Shop: At the ground
Opening Times: Matchdays only plus online sales
Telephone Nº: –

GROUND INFORMATION

Away Supporters' Entrances & Sections:
No usual segregation

ADMISSION INFO (2023/2024 PRICES)

Adult Standing/Seating: £17.00
Concessionary Standing/Seating: £12.00
19s-23s Standing/Seating: £10.00
Under-18s Standing/Seating: £7.00
Note: Under-14s must be accompanied by a paying adult

DISABLED INFORMATION

Wheelchairs: Accommodated
Helpers: Admitted
Prices: Concessionary prices apply for disabled fans Helpers are admitted free of charge.
Disabled Toilets: Available
Contact: (01895) 637487

Travelling Supporters' Information:
Routes: Exit the M25 at Junction 16 and take the A40 towards Uxbridge. At the Polish War Memorial Junction with the A4180, follow the Ruislip signs (West End Road). After about 1½ miles, turn right into Grosvenor Vale for the ground.

WOKING FC

Founded: 1889
Former Names: None
Nickname: 'Cardinals'
Ground: Laithwaite Community Stadium, Kingfield, Woking, Surrey GU22 9AA
Record Attendance: 6,064 (vs Coventry City, 1997)

Colours: Shirts are Red & White halves, Black shorts
Telephone Nº: (01483) 772470
Ground Capacity: 6,161
Seating Capacity: 2,511
Web site: www.wokingfc.co.uk
E-mail: admin@wokingfc.co.uk

GENERAL INFORMATION

Car Parking: Limited parking at the ground
Coach Parking: Please contact the club for details
Nearest Railway Station: Woking (1 mile)
Nearest Bus Station: Woking
Club Shop: At the ground
Opening Times: Tuesdays 1.00pm to 5.00pm, Thursdays 9.00am to 1.00pm and Matchdays
Telephone Nº: (01483) 772470 Extension 240

GROUND INFORMATION

Away Supporters' Entrances & Sections:
Kingfield Road entrance for the Chris Lane terrace

ADMISSION INFO (2023/2024 PRICES)

Adult Standing/Seating: £20.00
17s to 22s Standing/Seating: £12.00
Under-17s Standing/Seating : £8.00
Under-14s Standing/Seating: £5.00
Senior Citizen Standing/Seating: £15.00
Note: Prices are higher for tickets bought on the day.

DISABLED INFORMATION

Wheelchairs: 8 spaces in the Leslie Gosden Stand and 8 spaces in front of the Family Stand
Helpers: Admitted
Prices: Concessionary prices apply for disabled fans. Helpers are admitted free of charge
Disabled Toilets: Yes – in the Leslie Gosden Stand and Family Stand area
Contact: (01483) 772470 (Bookings are necessary)

Travelling Supporters' Information:
Routes: Exit the M25 at Junction 10 and follow the A3 towards Guildford. Leave at the next junction onto the B2215 through Ripley and join the A247 to Woking. Alternatively, exit the M25 at Junction 11 and follow the A320 to Woking Town Centre. The ground is on the outskirts of Woking – follow signs on the A320 and A247.

YORK CITY FC

Founded: 1922
Nickname: 'The Minstermen'
Ground: LNER Community Stadium,
Kathryn Avenue, Monks Cross Drive, Huntington,
York YO32 9AF
Ground Capacity (All Seats): 8,500

Record Attendance: 7,488 (vs Boston United, 2022)
Colours: Maroon shirts with White shorts
Telephone Nº: (01904) 624447
Web Site: www.yorkcityfootballclub.co.uk
E-mail: enquiries@yorkcityfootballclub.co.uk

GENERAL INFORMATION

Car Parking: The Monks Cross Park & Ride site has 400 spaces reserved for Matchday users but tickets need to be purchased in advance via the club's ticketing website. Other car parks at Monks Cross have a 2-hour maximumparking time which is strictly enforced
Coach Parking: By Police direction
Nearest Railway Station: York (3 miles)
Club Shop: At the ground
Opening Times: Weekdays 10.00am – 2.00pm (but closed on Mondays & Tuesdays); Saturday Matchdays 11.00am–3.00pm; Evening matches open from 4.00pm until 7.45pm.

GROUND INFORMATION

Away Supporters' Entrances & Sections:
Usually in West or North Stands depending upon expected attendance so please check with club.

ADMISSION INFO (2023/2024 PRICES)

Adult Seating: £23.00
Concessionary Seating: £18.00
Students under 25 Seating: £11.00
14s - 18s Seating: £11.00
8s - 13s Seating: £8.00
Under-7s Seating: Free with a paying adult
Note: Tickets bought in advance are £1.00 less.

DISABLED INFORMATION

Wheelchairs: Numerous
Helpers: One helper admitted per disabled person
Prices: Normal prices apply for disabled fans. Helpers free
Disabled Toilets: Available at entrance to the disabled area
Contact: (01904) 942232 (Bookings are necessary).
Bespoke Disabled Parking is available at the Stadium.

Travelling Supporters' Information:
Routes: The stadium is located within the Monks Cross Shopping Park which is located on the North Eastern outskirts of York close to the junction of the A64 and A1237. However, please read car parking details above for important information.

The Vanarama National League North

Address

4th Floor, 20 Waterloo Street,
Birmingham B2 5TB

Web site www.thenationalleague.org.uk

Clubs for the 2023/2024 Season

ALFRETON TOWN FC

Founded: 1959
Former Names: None
Nickname: 'Reds'
Ground: The Impact Arena, North Street, Alfreton, Derbyshire DE55 7FZ
Record Attendance: 5,023 vs Matlock Town (1960)

Colours: Red shirts and shorts
Telephone Nº: (01773) 830277
Ground Capacity: 3,600
Seating Capacity: 1,500
Web site: www.alfretontownfootballclub.com
E-mail: enquiries@alfretontownfootballclub.com

GENERAL INFORMATION

Car Parking: At the ground plus street parking
Coach Parking: Available close to the ground
Nearest Railway Station: Alfreton (½ mile)
Nearest Bus Station: Alfreton (5 minutes walk)
Club Shop: At the ground
Opening Times: Weekdays 9.00am to 3.00pm
Telephone Nº: (01773) 830277

GROUND INFORMATION

Away Supporters' Entrances & Sections:
'Tin End' terrace behind the North Street goal

ADMISSION INFO (2023/2024 PRICES)

Adult Standing: £15.00
Adult Seating: £15.00
Senior Citizen Standing/Seating: £10.00
Ages 16 to 21 Standing/Seating: £10.00
Under-16s Standing: £3.00 (with a paying adult)
Under-16s Seating: £3.00 (with a paying adult)

DISABLED INFORMATION

Wheelchairs: Accommodated in dedicated areas of the ground
Helpers: Admitted
Prices: Normal prices for disabled fans. Free for helpers
Disabled Toilets: Available in Zones 3 and 8
Contact: (01773) 830277 (Bookings are not necessary)

Travelling Supporters' Information:
Routes: Exit the M1 at Junction 28 and take the A38 signposted for Derby. After 2 miles take the sliproad onto the B600 then go right at the main road towards the town centre. After ½ mile turn left down North Street and the ground is on the right after 200 yards.

BANBURY UNITED FC

Founded: 1931
Former Names: Spencer Villa FC and Banbury Spencer FC
Nickname: 'The Puritans'
Ground: The Banbury Plant Hire Community Stadium, Station Approach, Banbury OX16 5AB
Record Attendance: 7,160 (vs Oxford City – 1948)

Colours: Red and Gold shirts with Red shorts
Telephone Nº: (01295) 263354
Ground Capacity: 4,500
Seating Capacity: 250
Web site: www.banburyunited.co.uk

GENERAL INFORMATION

Car Parking: At the ground (up to 200 spaces)
Coach Parking: At the ground
Nearest Railway Station: Banbury (adjacent)
Nearest Bus Station: Banbury
Club Shop: At the ground
Opening Times: Matchdays only
Telephone Nº: (01295) 263354

GROUND INFORMATION

Away Supporters' Entrances & Sections:
No usual segregation

ADMISSION INFO (2023/2024 PRICES)

Adult Standing: £15.00
Adult Seating: £15.00
Senior Citizen Standing: £11.00
Senior Citizen Seating: £11.00
Under-18s Standing/Seating: £5.00
Under-11s Standing/Seating: £2.00

DISABLED INFORMATION

Wheelchairs: 6 spaces available in total
Helpers: Admitted
Prices: Normal prices apply
Disabled Toilets: Available
Contact: (01295) 263354

Travelling Supporters' Information:
Routes: Exit the M40 at Junction 11 and head towards Banbury. Go straight on at the first roundabout then left at the next into Concorde Avenue. Continue straight on at the next roundabout then turn left at the traffic lights. Take the 1st turning on the right into Station Approach then take the single track road on the extreme right of the Station which leads to the Stadium.

BISHOP'S STORTFORD FC

Founded: 1874
Former Names: None
Nickname: 'Blues' 'Bishops'
Ground: The R & D Advisors Stadium, Woodside Park, Dunmow Road, Bishop's Stortford CM23 5RG
Record Attendance: 3,555 (2000)

Colours: Blue shirts and shorts
Telephone Nº: (01279) 306456
Ground Capacity: 4,000
Seating Capacity: 225
Web site: www.bsfc.co.uk

GENERAL INFORMATION

Car Parking: 150 spaces available at the ground
Coach Parking: At the ground (bookings required)
Nearest Railway Station: Bishop's Stortford
Nearest Bus Station: Bishop's Stortford
Club Shop: At the ground
Opening Times: Matchdays only 1.30pm to 5.00pm
Telephone Nº: (01279) 306456

GROUND INFORMATION

Away Supporters' Entrances & Sections:
No usual segregation

ADMISSION INFO (2023/2024 PRICES)

Adult Standing/Seating: £12.00
Concessionary Standing/Seating: £8.00
Student Standing/Seating: £6.00
Under-16s Standing/Seating: £1.00
Note: Under-12s are admitted free of charge when accompanied by a paying adult.

DISABLED INFORMATION

Wheelchairs: Accommodated in the disabled section
Helpers: Admitted
Prices: Free of charge for the disabled and helpers
Disabled Toilets: Yes
Contact: (01279) 306456 (Bookings are not necessary)

Travelling Supporters' Information:
Routes: Exit the M11 at junction 8 and take the A1250 towards Bishop Stortford. Turn left at the first roundabout and the ground is first right opposite the Golf Club (the entrance is between Industrial Units).

BLYTH SPARTANS AFC

Founded: 1899
Former Names: None
Nickname: 'Spartans'
Ground: Croft Park, Blyth, Northumberland, NE24 3JE
Record Attendance: 10,186 (1956)

Colours: Green and White striped shirts, Black shorts
Telephone Nº: (01670) 352373 (Office)
Ground Capacity: 4,435
Seating Capacity: 556
Web site: www.blythspartans.com
E-mail: generalmanager@blythspartans.com

GENERAL INFORMATION

Car Parking: At the ground
Coach Parking: At the ground
Nearest Railway Station: Newcastle
Nearest Bus Station: Blyth (5 minutes walk)
Club Shop: At the ground
Opening Times: Matchdays only
Telephone Nº: (01670) 352373

GROUND INFORMATION

Away Supporters' Entrances & Sections:
No usual segregation

ADMISSION INFO (2023/2024 PRICES)

Adult Standing: £15.00
Adult Seating: £17.00
Senior Citizen Standing: £9.00
Senior Citizen Seating: £11.00
Ages 11 to 16 & Student Standing: £6.00
Ages 11 to 16 & Student Seating: £8.00
Note: Under-11s are admitted free of charge when accompanied by a paying adult

DISABLED INFORMATION

Wheelchairs: 3 elevated wheelchair spaces available
Helpers: Please phone the club for information
Prices: Adult disabled fans are charged the Senior Citizen rate shown above. Younger disabled fans charged lower rate.
Disabled Toilets: Available adjacent to the Main Stand
Contact: (01670) 352373 (Bookings are necessary)

Travelling Supporters' Information:
Routes: Pass through the Tyne Tunnel and take the left lane for Morpeth (A19/A1). At the 2nd roundabout (after approximately 7 miles) take full right turn for the A189 (signposted Ashington). After 2 miles take the slip road (A1061 signposted Blyth). Follow signs for Blyth turning left at the caravan site. At the 2nd roundabout turn right and the ground is on the left.

BOSTON UNITED FC

Founded: 1933
Former Names: Boston Town FC & Boston Swifts FC
Nickname: 'The Pilgrims'
Ground: The Jakemans Community Stadium, Pilgrim Way, Wyberton, Boston PE21 7NE
Ground Capacity: 5,000
Seating Capacity: 2,400
Record Attendance: 2,694 (vs King's Lynn Town FC)

Colours: Amber and Black shirts, Black shorts
Telephone Nº: (01205) 364406 (Office)
Matchday Info: (01205) 364406
Web Site: www.bostonunited.co.uk
E-mail: karen.houlden@bufc.co.uk

GENERAL INFORMATION

Car Parking: At the ground
Coach Parking: At the ground
Nearest Railway Station: Boston (1 mile)
Nearest Bus Station: Boston Coach Station
Club Shop: At the ground
Opening Times: Weekdays and Saturday Matchdays from 9.00am to 5.00pm
Telephone Nº: (01205) 364406

GROUND INFORMATION

Away Supporters' Entrances & Sections:
Accommodation in the Main Stand for matches where segregation is in force

ADMISSION INFO (2023/2024 PRICES)

Adult Standing: £15.00
Adult Seating: £17.00
Child Standing: £6.00
Child Seating: £7.00
Senior Citizen Standing: £12.00
Senior Citizen Seating: £13.00
Note: Discounted family tickets may be available. Please contact the club for further information.

DISABLED INFORMATION

Wheelchairs: Accommodated in the Main Stand
Helpers: One helper admitted per disabled fan
Prices: £12.00 for disabled fans using wheelchairs. Free of charge for helpers
Disabled Toilets: Available
Contact: (01205) 364406 (Bookings are necessary)

Travelling Supporters' Information:
The Jakemans Community Stadium is located by the side of the A16 on the outskirts of Wyberton which is just to the south of Boston. The Stadium is clearly signposted from the A16.

BRACKLEY TOWN FC

Founded: 1890
Former Names: None
Nickname: 'Saints'
Ground: St. James Park, Churchill Way, Brackley, NN13 7EJ
Record Attendance: 2,604 (12th May 2013)
Colours: Red and White shirts with White shorts
Telephone N°: (01280) 704077
Ground Capacity: 3,500
Seating Capacity: 300
Web Site: www.brackleytownfc.com
E-mail: janenebutters@brackleytownfc.co.uk

GENERAL INFORMATION

Car Parking: At the ground (£2.00 charge per car)
Coach Parking: At the ground
Nearest Railway Station: King's Sutton (6¾ miles)
Club Shop: At the ground
Opening Times: Matchdays and by appointment only
Telephone N°: (01280) 704077

GROUND INFORMATION

Away Supporters' Entrances & Sections:
Accommodation in the Cricket Ground end for games when segregation is in force

ADMISSION INFO (2023/2024 PRICES)

Adult Standing/Seating: £17.00
Concessions Standing/Seating: £12.00
Under-18s Standing/Seating: £7.00
Under-10s Seating/Seating: £4.00
Under-5s Seating/Standing: £2.00
Note: Tickets bought in advance are cheaper.

DISABLED INFORMATION

Wheelchairs: Accommodated
Helpers: Admitted
Prices: Normal prices apply for the disabled. Free for helpers
Disabled Toilets: Available
Contact: (01280) 704077 (Bookings are necessary)

Travelling Supporters' Information:
Routes: From the West: Take the A422 to Brackley and take the first exit at the roundabout with the junction of the A43, heading north into Oxford Road.* Go straight on at the next roundabout and continue into Bridge Street before turning right into Churchill Way. The ground is located at the end of the road; From the South: Take the A43 northwards to Brackley. Take the second exit at the roundabout with the junction of the A422 and head into Oxford Road. Then as from * above; From the North-East: Take the A43 to Brackley. Upon reaching Brackley, take the 1st exit at the 1st roundabout, the 2nd exit at the next roundabout then the 3rd exit at the following roundabout into Oxford Road. Then as from * above.

BUXTON FC

Founded: 1877
Former Names: None
Nickname: 'The Bucks'
Ground: The Tarmac Stadium, Silverlands, Buxton SK17 6QH
Record Attendance: 6,000 (1951/52 season)

Colours: Royal Blue shirts and shorts
Telephone Nº: (01298) 601137
Ground Capacity: 4,000
Seating Capacity: 490
Web Site: www.buxtonfc.co.uk
E-mail: chris@buxtonfc.co.uk

GENERAL INFORMATION

Car Parking: Limited number of spaces at the ground
Coach Parking: At the ground
Nearest Railway Station: Buxton (¾ mile)
Club Shop: At the ground
Opening Times: Matchdays only

GROUND INFORMATION

Away Supporters' Entrances & Sections:
No usual segregation

ADMISSION INFO (2023/2024 PRICES)

Adult Standing/Seating: £15.00
Concessionary Standing/Seating: £10.00
16s to 21s Standing/Seating: £5.00
Under-16s Standing/Seating: £2.00

DISABLED INFORMATION

Wheelchairs: Accommodated
Helpers: Admitted
Prices: Normal prices apply for the disabled and helpers
Disabled Toilets: Available
Contact: (01298) 601137 (Bookings are not necessary)

Travelling Supporters' Information:
Routes: From Matlock/Bakewell: Take the A6 to Buxton then turn left at the roundabout by Safeway onto the B5059 (signposted Poole's Cavern). Take the first right into Peveril Road, turn left at the T-junction into Cliff Mill and continue into Clifton Road. Turn right at the T-junction into Silverlands and the ground is on the right; From Leek/Macclesfield: Take the A53 to Buxton and turn right onto the B5059 Macclesfield Road at the edge of town. Continue along the B5059, crossing the A515 into Dale Road (still B5059), then take the 6th turning on the left into Peveril Road. Then as above; From Manchester: Take the A6 to Buxton, turn left at the mini-roundabout junction with the A53 continuing up the A6 Bakewell Road. Turn right at the mini-roundabout by Safeway into B5059 Dale Road. Then as above.

CHESTER FC

Founded: 1885
Former Names: Chester FC and Chester City FC
Nickname: 'Blues'
Ground: Swansway Chester Stadium, Bumpers Lane, Chester CH1 4LT
Ground Capacity: 6,500
Seating Capacity: 4,170

Record Attendance: 5,987 (17th April 2004)
Colours: Blue and White striped shirts, White shorts
Ground Telephone Nº: (01244) 371376
Ticket Office: (01244) 371376
Web site: www.chesterfc.com
E-mail: info@chesterfc.com

GENERAL INFORMATION

Car Parking: Ample spaces available at the ground (£2.00)
Coach Parking: Available at the ground
Nearest Railway Station: Chester (2 miles)
Nearest Bus Station: Chester (1½ miles)
Club Shop: At the ground
Opening Times: Weekdays & matchdays 10.00am–4.00pm
Telephone Nº: (01244) 371376

GROUND INFORMATION

Away Supporters' Entrances & Sections:
South Stand for covered seating and also part of the West Stand

ADMISSION INFO (2023/2024 PRICES)

Adult Standing: £15.00 **Adult Seating**: £17.00
Concessionary Standing: £13.00 **Seating**: £14.00
Ages 18 to 21 Standing: £11.00 **Seating**: £12.00
Ages 12 to 17 Seating/Standing: £4.00
Under-12s: Free of charge

DISABLED INFORMATION

Wheelchairs: 40 spaces for wheelchairs in the West Stand and East Stand
Helpers: Admitted
Prices: Normal prices for the disabled. Free for helpers
Disabled Toilets: Available in West and East Stands
Contact: (01244) 371376 (Bookings are necessary)
Bob Marsden (Liaison) – bobbymarsden259@gmail.com

Travelling Supporters' Information:
Routes: From the North: Take the M56, A41 or A56 into the Town Centre and then follow Queensferry (A548) signs into Sealand Road. Turn left at the traffic lights by 'Tesco' into Bumpers Lane – the ground is ½ mile at the end of the road; From the East: Take the A54 or A51 into the Town Centre (then as North); From the South: Take the A41 or A483 into Town Centre (then as North); From the West: Take the A55, A494 or A548 and follow Queensferry signs towards Birkenhead (A494) and after 1¼ miles bear left onto the A548 (then as North); From the M6/M56 (Avoiding Town Centre): Take the M56 to Junction 16 (signposted Queensferry), turn left at the roundabout onto A5117, signposted Wales. At the next roundabout turn left onto the A5480 (signposted Chester) and after approximately 3 miles take the 3rd exit from the roundabout (signposted Sealand Road Industrial Parks). Go straight across 2 sets of traffic lights into Bumpers Lane. The ground is ½ mile on the right.

CHORLEY FC

Founded: 1883
Former Names: None
Nickname: 'Magpies'
Ground: Victory Park Stadium, Duke Street, Chorley, PR7 3DU
Record Attendance: 9,679 (v Darwen 15/11/1932)
Colours: Black & White striped shirts with Black shorts
Telephone Nº: (01257) 230007
Ground Capacity: 4,100
Seating Capacity: 980
Web site: www.chorleyfc.com
E-mail: commercial@chorleyfc.com

GENERAL INFORMATION

Car Parking: Pilling Lane (£3.00)
Coach Parking: At the ground
Nearest Railway Station: Chorley (¼ mile)
Nearest Bus Station: 15 minutes from the ground
Club Shop: At the ground
Opening Times: Weekdays 12.00pm to 2.00pm and Matchdays 12.00pm until kick-off.
Telephone Nº: (01257) 230007

GROUND INFORMATION

Away Supporters' Entrances & Sections:
Pilling Lane Stand entrances and accommodation

ADMISSION INFO (2023/2024 PRICES)

Adult Standing: £15.00
Adult Seating: £15.00
Concessionary Standing/Seating: £12.00
Ages 18 to 21 Standing/Seating: £7.00
Ages 12 to 17 Standing/Seating: £5.00
Under-12s Standing/Seating: Free of charge but must be accompanied by an adult

DISABLED INFORMATION

Wheelchairs: Accommodated by prior arrangement
Helpers: Admitted
Prices: Normal prices for disabled fans. Helpers free of charge
Disabled Toilets: Available in the Social Club
Contact: (01257) 230007 (Bookings are not necessary)

Travelling Supporters' Information:
Routes: Exit the M61 at Junction 6 and follow the A6 to Chorley. Going past the Yarrow Bridge Hotel on Bolton Road, turn left at the 1st set of traffic lights into Pilling Lane. Take the 1st right into Ashby Street and the ground is the 2nd entrance on the left; Alternative Route: Exit the M6 at Junction 27 and follow signs to Chorley. Turn left at the lights and continue down the A49 for 2½ miles before turning right onto B5251. On entering Chorley, turn right into Duke Street 200 yards past The Plough.

CURZON ASHTON FC

Founded: 1963
Former Names: None
Nickname: 'The Nash'
Ground: Tameside Stadium, Richmond Street, Ashton-under-Lyne OL7 9HG
Record Attendance: 3,210 (2007)

Colours: Royal Blue shirts and shorts
Telephone Nº: (0161) 330-6033
Ground Capacity: 4,000
Seating Capacity: 527
Web Site: www.curzon-ashton.co.uk
E-mail: office@curzon-ashton.co.uk

GENERAL INFORMATION

Car Parking: At the ground
Coach Parking: At the ground
Nearest Railway Station: Ashton-under-Lyne (1 mile)
Club Shop: At the ground
Opening Times: Matchdays only
Telephone Nº: (0161) 330-6033

GROUND INFORMATION

Away Supporters' Entrances & Sections:
No usual segregation

ADMISSION INFO (2023/2024 PRICES)

Adult Standing/Seating: £15.00
Senior Citizen Standing/Seating: £10.00
16s to 18s Standing/Seating: £5.00.
Under-16s Standing/Seating: Free with a paying adult

DISABLED INFORMATION

Wheelchairs: Accommodated
Helpers: Admitted
Prices: Normal prices apply for the disabled and helpers
Disabled Toilets: Available
Contact: (0161) 330-6033 (Bookings are not necessary)

Travelling Supporters' Information:
Routes: Exit the M60 at Junction 23 and take the A6140 signposted for Ashton. Continue along the A6140 to the set of traffic lights with a Cinema on the right then turn left. Cross over a bridge and go straight across the mini-roundabout before turning left into the ground.

DARLINGTON FC

Founded: 1883 (Re-formed 2012)
Former Names: Successor to the club Darlington FC, formed as Darlington 1883 and renamed in 2017
Nickname: 'Darlo', 'The Quakers'
Ground: Blackwell Meadows, Grange Road, Darlington DL1 5NR
Ground Capacity: 3,100 **Seating Capacity**: 588

Record Attendance: 3,000 (26th December 2016)
Colours: Black and White hooped shirts, Black shorts
Contact Telephone Nº: 01432 268257
Web Site: www.darlingtonfc.co.uk
E-mail: dave.watson@darlingtonfc.org

GENERAL INFORMATION

Car Parking: A limited number of spaces at Blackwell Meadows are available on a first-come, first-served basis with a £5.00 fee. Alternatively, use town centre car parks (1½ miles)
Coach Parking: Limited parking at the ground
Nearest Railway Station: Darlington (1½ miles)
Nearest Bus Station: Darlington Town Centre (1½ miles)
Club Shop: Quaker Retail at the Dolphin Centre, Darlington and at Mysportswear, Morton Park, Darlington
Opening Times: Weekdays 10.00am to 1.00pm.
Telephone Nº: 07488 564642 (Quaker Retail) and (01325) 488884 (Mysportswear)

GROUND INFORMATION

Away Supporters' Entrances & Sections:
Western End of the ground when segregation is in force

ADMISSION INFO (2023/2024 PRICES)

Adult Standing: £15.00
Adult Seating: £17.00
Concessionary Standing: £11.00
Concessionary Seating: £13.00
Under-18s Standing: £5.00
Under-18s Seating: £7.00
Under-12s Standing/Seating: Free of charge when accompanied by a paying adult (£2.00 in seats)

DISABLED INFORMATION

Wheelchairs: Accommodated
Helpers: Helpers are admitted
Prices: Concessionary prices for the disabled and helpers
Disabled Toilets: Available
Contact: dave.watson@darlingtonfc.org (Bookings are necessary)

Travelling Supporters' Information:
Routes: From the South: Exit the A1(M) at Junction 57 and take the A66(M) towards Darlington. At the end of the motorway, continue onto the A66 and take the second exit at the next roundabout onto the A167 Darlington Road. Blackwell Meadows is on the right after 400 yards; From the North: Exit the A1(M) at Junction 59 and take the A167 to Darlington. Upon entering Darlington, continue along the A167, taking the second exit at the roundabout into North Road, the first exit at Northgate Roundabout onto St. Cuthbert's Way then following the road around around Darlington town centre into Victoria Road before turning left at the Baptist church into Grange Road. Blackwell Meadows in on the left after approximately 1 mile.

FARSLEY CELTIC AFC

Founded: 1908 (Original club)
Former Names: Farsley Celtic FC
Nickname: 'Villagers'
Ground: The Citadel, Newlands, Farsley, Leeds, LS28 5BE
Record Attendance: 2,462 (2006)

Colours: White and Green hooped shirts with Green shorts
Ground Capacity: 4,000
Seating Capacity: 300
Web site: www.farsleyceltic.com
E-mail: office@farsleyceltic.com

GENERAL INFORMATION

Car Parking: Available at the ground (70 spaces)
Coach Parking: Available at the ground
Nearest Railway Station: New Pudsey (1 mile)
Nearest Bus Station: Pudsey (1 mile)
Club Shop: At the ground
Opening Times: Weekday evenings 6.00pm – 11.00pm and weekends noon until 11.00pm
Telephone Nº: 07736 037604

GROUND INFORMATION

Away Supporters' Entrances & Sections:
No usual segregation

ADMISSION INFO (2023/2024 PRICES)

Adult Standing: £15.00
Adult Seating: £15.00
Senior Citizen/Student/Under-18s Standing: £10.00
Senior Citizen/Student/Under-18s Seating: £10.00
Juniors (11 - 16): £6.00
Children (4 - 10): £3.00 (with paying adult)
Under 4s: Free with a paying adult

DISABLED INFORMATION

Wheelchairs: Accommodated
Helpers: Please phone the club for information
Prices: Please phone the club for information
Disabled Toilets: Available
Contact: office@farsleyceltic.com (Bookings are necessary)

Travelling Supporters' Information:
Routes: From the North: Take the A1 to Wetherby then the A58 to Leeds. After about 8 miles take the 3rd exit at the roundabout onto the A6120 Ring Road. Follow signs for Bradford for approximately 12 miles and at the 7th roundabout take the B6157 signposted Stanningley. Continue for ½ mile passing the Police Station on the left then turn left down New Street (at the Tradex Warehouse). Turn right into Newlands and the ground is situated at the end of the road next to a new housing development.

GLOUCESTER CITY FC

Founded: 1883
Former Names: Gloucester YMCA
Nickname: 'The Tigers'
Ground: Tigerturf Stadium, Sudmeadow Road, Hempsted, Gloucester GL2 5HD
Record Attendance: 8,326 (1956)

Colours: Yellow & Red Banded shirts with Black shorts
Telephone Nº: None
Ground Capacity: 4,000
Seating Capacity: 700
Web site: www.gloucestercityafc.com
E-mail: secretary@gcafc.co.uk

GENERAL INFORMATION

Car Parking: At the ground for disabled only, however free parking is available in Sainsbury's car park which is a 5 min. walk from St Ann Way (satnav GL2 5SA)
Nearest Railway Station: Gloucester (1 mile)
Nearest Bus Station: Gloucester
Club Shop: At the ground
Opening Times: Matchdays only

GROUND INFORMATION

Away Supporters' Entrances & Sections:
No usual segregation

ADMISSION INFO (2023/2024 PRICES)

Adult Standing/Seating: £15.00 (on the day)
Cocessions Standing/Seating: £12.00 (on the day)
Under-16s Standing/Seating: £5.00 (on the day)
Under-11s: Admitted free of charge with a paying adult
Note: Ticket prices are £2.00 cheaper if pre-booked

DISABLED INFORMATION

Wheelchairs: Accommodated
Helpers: Admitted
Prices: Normal prices apply for disabled fans
Disabled Toilets: Available
Contact: secretary@gtafc.co.uk (Bookings are necessary)

Travelling Supporters' Information:
Routes: Take the A40 into the City Centre towards the Historic Docks, then take Severn Road and turn right into Hempstead Lane. Take the second right into Sudmeadow Road and the ground is 50 yards on the left.

HEREFORD FC

Founded: 2014
Former Names: The club is a successor to Hereford Utd FC which was formed in 1924
Nickname: 'United' 'The Bulls'
Ground: Edgar Street, Hereford HR4 9JU
Record Attendance: 18,114 (4th January 1958)

Colours: White shirts with Black shorts
Telephone Nº: (01432) 268257
Ground Capacity: 5,213
Seating Capacity: 3,390
Web site: www.herefordfc.co.uk
E-mail: info@herefordfc.co.uk

GENERAL INFORMATION

Car Parking: Merton Meadow Car Park (Near the ground)
Coach Parking: Merton Meadow Car Park
Nearest Railway Station: Hereford (½ mile)
Nearest Bus Station: Commercial Road, Hereford
Club Shop: At the ground
Opening Times: Wednesday and Friday 10.00am – 4.00pm. Midweek home games, 10.00am–4.00pm & 6.00pm–7.30pm, Saturday Matchdays 12.00pm to 2.45pm.
Telephone Nº: (01432) 268257

GROUND INFORMATION

Away Supporters' Entrances & Sections:
Edgar Street entrances for the Len Weston Stand and Terrace

ADMISSION INFO (2023/2024 PRICES)

Adult Standing: £18.00
Adult Seating: £21.00
Ages 16 to 18 Standing: £11.00
Ages 16 to 18 Seating: £12.00
Under-16s Standing/Seating: £5.00 (Under-5s free)
Concessionary Standing: £16.00
Concessionary Seating: £18.00
Note: Pre-booked tickets are cheaper

DISABLED INFORMATION

Wheelchairs: 7 spaces in total for Home and Away fans
Helpers: One helper admitted per disabled person
Prices: Concessionary prices for the disabled. Free for helpers
Disabled Toilets: Available in the Merton Stand
Contact: (01432) 268257

Travelling Supporters' Information:
Routes: From the North: Follow A49 Hereford signs straight into Edgar Street; From the East: Take the A465 or A438 into Hereford Town Centre, then follow signs for Leominster (A49) into Edgar Street; From the South: Take the A49 or A45 into the Town Centre (then as East); From the West: Take the A438 into the Town Centre (then as East).

KING'S LYNN TOWN FC

Founded: 1879
Former Names: Lynn Town FC, Lynn FC
Nickname: 'The Linnets'
Ground: The Walks Stadium, Tennyson Road, King's Lynn PE30 5PB
Record Attendance: 12,937 (vs Exeter City 1950/51)

Colours: Blue shirts with Yellow trim, Blue shorts
Telephone Nº: (01553) 760060
Ground Capacity: 8,200
Seating Capacity: 1,200
Web site: www.kltown.co.uk
E-mail: office@kltown.co.uk

GENERAL INFORMATION

Car Parking: 40 spaces available at the ground
Coach Parking: At the ground
Nearest Railway Station: King's Lynn (¼ mile)
Nearest Bus Station: King's Lynn (¼ mile)
Club Shop: At the ground
Opening Times: Matchdays only
Telephone Nº: (01553) 760060

GROUND INFORMATION

Away Supporters' Entrances & Sections:
No usual segregation but away fans should use the North East Corner when segregation is in force.

ADMISSION INFO (2023/2024 PRICES)

Adult Standing: £18.00
Adult Seating: £20.00 – £23.00
Concessions Standing: £16.00
Concessions Seating: £18.00 – £23.00
Under-16s Standing: £5.00
Under-16s Seating: £5.00 - £11.00 (except Premium seats)

DISABLED INFORMATION

Wheelchairs: Accommodated
Helpers: Please phone the club for information
Prices: Please phone the club for information
Disabled Toilets: Available
Contact: (01553) 760060 (Bookings are not necessary)

Travelling Supporters' Information:
Routes: From all directions: The A47/A17/A10 all meet at Hardwick Roundabout. At this roundabout follow signs for the town centre passing through two sets of traffic lights. After the second set of lights get in the right hand lane and take the 4th exit at the roundabout keeping the Car Sales outlet on the left. Continue for ½ mile into Tennyson Road and the ground is situated on the left hand side.

PETERBOROUGH SPORTS FC

Founded: 1908
Former Names: Brotherhood Engineering Works FC and Bearings Direct FC
Nickname: 'The Turbines'
Ground: Pims Park, 651 Lincoln Road, Peterborough PE1 3HA
Ground Capacity: 3,016
Seating Capacity: 800

Record Attendance: 790 (2021/2022 season)
Colours: Orange & Black shirts and shorts
Telephone N°: 07913 761312
Web site: www.pslfc.com
E-mail: hrcdarren@gmail.com

GENERAL INFORMATION

Car Parking: Available at ground
Coach Parking: Contact Club
Nearest Railway Station: Peterborough (2mls)

GROUND INFORMATION

Away Supporters' Entrances & Sections:
No segregation normally but check the club website for details of matches when this is required.

ADMISSION INFO (2023/2024 PRICES)

Adult Standing/Seating: £16.00
Concessions Standing/Seating: £12.00
Student Standing/Seating: £8.00
13s to 17s Standing/Seating: £8.00
Under-13s Standing/Seating: Free with a paying Adult

DISABLED INFORMATION

Wheelchairs: 4 spaces are available
Helpers: Admitted
Prices: Normal prices apply for disabled supporters. Helpers are admitted free of charge
Disabled Toilets: Yes
Contact: (Bookings are recommended)

Travelling Supporters' Information:
Routes: The ground is located off the A47 (Soke Parkway) in Peterborough close to the junction with the A15. Exit Soke Parkway at turnoff 18 and head southward along the A15 (Bourges Boulevard). After approximately 400 yards take the slip road to the left before the traffic lights then, at the T-junction, turn right into Lincoln Road then, after 600 yards, turn left for the ground.

RUSHALL OLYMPIC FC

Founded: 1893 (Re-formed in 1951)
Former Names: None
Nickname: 'The Pics'
Ground: Dales Lane, off Daw End Lane, Rushall, near Walsall WS4 1LJ
Record Attendance: 2,000

Colours: Gold and Black shirts with Black shorts
Telephone Nº: (01922) 641021
Ground Capacity: 2,500
Seating Capacity: 200
Web Site: www.rofc.co.uk

GENERAL INFORMATION

Car Parking: At the ground (parking charge £2.00)
Coach Parking: At the ground
Nearest Railway Station: Walsall (3¼ miles)
Club Shop: At the ground
Opening Times: Matchdays only
Telephone Nº: –

GROUND INFORMATION

Away Supporters' Entrances & Sections:
No usual segregation

ADMISSION INFO (2023/2024 PRICES)

Adult Standing/Seating: £14.00
Concessions Standing/Seating: £10.00
12s to 16s Standing/Seating: £5.50
Under 12s Standing/Seating: £1.50

DISABLED INFORMATION

Wheelchairs: Accommodated
Helpers: Admitted
Prices: Normal prices apply for the disabled and helpers
Disabled Toilets: Available
Contact: (01922) 641021 (Bookings are not necessary)

Travelling Supporters' Information:
Routes: Exit the M6 at Junction 9 and take the A454 then the A4148 towards Walsall. Turn left onto the A461 Lichfield Street at the roundabout then take the first exit at the next roundabout continuing on A461 Lichfield Road. Pass underneath the railway bridge then turn right onto the B4154 into Daw End Lane. Cross the Rushall Canal and the entrance to the ground is on the right hand side of the road.

SCARBOROUGH ATHLETIC FC

Founded: 2007
Former Names: The club was founded following the demise of Scarborough FC
Nickname: 'Seadogs'
Ground: Flamingo Land Stadium, Scarborough Sports Village, Ashburn Road, Scarborough YO11 2JW

Colours: Red shirts and shorts
Email: info@scarboroughathleticfc.com
Ground Capacity: 3,252
Seating Capacity: 586
Web site: www.scarboroughathletic.com

GENERAL INFORMATION

Car Parking: 200 Space Car Park at the Stadium
Coach Parking: 1 space at the Stadium
Nearest Railway Station: Scarborough Central (1 mile)
Nearest Bus Station: Town Centre (1 miles)
Club Shop: Online

GROUND INFORMATION

Away Supporters' Entrances & Sections:
Swimming Pool End

ADMISSION INFO (2023/2024 PRICES)

Adult Standing: £15.00
Adult Seating: £17.00
Concessions Standing: £11.00
Concessions Seating: £13.00
12s to 17s Standing/Seating: £7.00
Under-12s): £1.00 with a paying adult/concession

DISABLED INFORMATION

Wheelchairs:Accommodated
Helpers: One helper admitted per wheelchair
Prices: Normal prices for the wheelchair disabled. Free of charge for helpers
Disabled Toilets: Available
Contact: Shaun Tymon

Travelling Supporters' Information:
Routes: Follow the A64 into Scarborough passing the Park & Ride, Lidl and Peugot Garage before coming to a set of traffic lights. Turn right into Valley Road, continue straight on at the roundabout then take the next right into Ashburn Road. The Stadium is at the end of the road.

SCUNTHORPE UNITED FC

Founded: 1899
Former Name: Scunthorpe and Lindsey United FC (1899-1912)
Nickname: 'The Iron'
Ground: Glanford Park, Jack Brownsword Way, Scunthorpe DN15 8TD
Ground Capacity: 9,088 **Seating Capacity**: 6,322

Record Attendance: 9,077 (22nd September 2010)
Colours: Blue shirt with Claret trim, Blue shorts
Telephone Nº: (01724) 747670
Ticket Office: (01724) 747670 (www.sufctickets.com)
Web Site: www.scunthorpe-united.co.uk
E-mail: receptionist@scunthorpe-united.co.uk

GENERAL INFORMATION

Car Parking: Spaces for 600 cars at the ground (£3.00)
Coach Parking: At the ground
Nearest Railway Station: Scunthorpe (1½ miles)
Nearest Bus Station: Scunthorpe (1½ miles)
Club Shop: At the ground
Opening Times: Weekdays 8.30am to 5.00pm
Matchdays 9.00am to 3.00pm and 4.45pm to 5.15pm
Telephone Nº: (01724) 849344

GROUND INFORMATION

Away Supporters' Entrances & Sections:
Turnstiles 6-7 for the South Stand (AMS Stand)

ADMISSION INFO (2023/2024 PRICES)

Adult Standing: £16.00 – £22.00
Adult Seating: £21.00 – £26.00
Concessionary Standing: £12.00 – £18.00
Concessionary Seating: £14.00 – £18.00
Under-18s Standing: £5.00 – £9.00 (Under-12s free)
Under-18s Seating: £5.00 – £9.00
Note: Prices depend on match category & advance purchase

FANS WITH DISABILITIES INFORMATION

Wheelchairs: 10 spaces for Home fans and 6 spaces for Away fans in designated section of the Clugston Stand
Helpers: One helper admitted per fan with disabilities
Prices: Normal prices for fans with disabilities. One helper admitted free per fan requiring medium to higher rate of care.
Disabled Toilets: Available
Commentaries are available for the blind
Contact: (01724) 747670 (Bookings are necessary)

Travelling Supporters' Information:
Routes: From All Parts: Exit the M180 at Junction 3 onto the M181. Follow the M181 to the roundabout with the A18 and take the A18 towards Scunthorpe – the ground is on the right after 200 yards.

SOUTHPORT FC

Founded: 1881
Former Names: Southport Vulcan FC, Southport Central FC
Nickname: 'The Sandgrounders' and 'The Port'
Ground: The Big Help Stadium, Haig Avenue, Southport, Merseyside PR8 6JZ
Record Attendance: 20,010 (vs Newcastle, 1932)

Colours: Yellow shirts with Black shorts
Telephone Nº: (01704) 533422
Ground Capacity: 6,008
Seating Capacity: 1,660
Web site: www.southportfc.net

GENERAL INFORMATION

Car Parking: Street parking
Coach Parking: Adjacent to the ground
Nearest Railway Station: Meols Cop (½ mile)
Nearest Bus Station: Southport Town Centre
Club Shop: At the ground
Opening Times: Matchdays from 11.00am (from 6.30pm on evening matchdays)
Telephone Nº: (01704) 533422

GROUND INFORMATION

Away Supporters' Entrances & Sections:
The George Roberts Terrace

ADMISSION INFO (2023/2024 PRICES)

Adult Standing: £13.50
Adult Seating: £15.00
Concessionary Standing: £10.00
Concessionary Seating: £11.00
12s to 17s Standing/Seating: £5.00/£6.00
Note: Children aged 11 and under are admitted free of charge when accompanied by a paying adult.

DISABLED INFORMATION

Wheelchairs: Accommodated in front of the Grandstand
Helpers: Admitted
Prices: Normal prices charged for the disabled. Helpers are admitted free of charge
Disabled Toilets: Available at the Blowick End of the Grandstand
Contact: (01704) 533422 (Bookings are not necessary)

Travelling Supporters' Information:
Routes: Exit the M58 at Junction 3 and take the A570 to Southport. At the major roundabout (McDonalds/Tesco) go straight on into Scarisbrick New Road, pass over the brook and turn right into Haig Avenue at the traffic lights. The ground is then on the right-hand side.

SOUTH SHIELDS FC

Founded: 1899 (refounded in 1974)
Former Names: None
Nickname: 'Mariners'
Ground: 1st Cloud Arena, Mariners Park, Shaftesbury Avenue, South Shields NE32 3UP
Ground Capacity: 4,000
Seating Capacity: 1,100

Record Attendance: 3,464 (2017)
Web site: www.southshieldsfc.co.uk
Colours: Claret & Blue shirts with White shorts
Telephone N°: (0191) 454-7800
E-mail: via the 'Contact' section of the website

GENERAL INFORMATION

Car Parking: At stadium and overflow car parking at the nearby Barbour Store.
Coach Parking: By Police Direction
Nearest Railway Station: Bede Metro Station (6 mins walk)
Club Shop: Online via website.

GROUND INFORMATION

Away Supporters' Entrances & Sections:
Sima Shed End

ADMISSION INFO (2023/2024 PRICES)

Adult Standing/Seating: £15.00
Senior Citizen/Student Standing/Seating: £10.00
12s to 16s Standing/Seating: £5.00
Under-12s Standing/Seating: £3.00
Note: Prices are cheaper for prior online purchase.

DISABLED INFORMATION

Wheelchairs: Accommodated
Prices: Normal prices apply for disabled supporters. Helpers are admitted free of charge
Disabled Toilets: Yes
Contact: (0191) 454-7800 (Bookings are necessary)

Travelling Supporters' Information:
Routes: Take the A1(M) to the A194(M) at Washington and continue past the A184 towards the Port of Tyne (Leam Lane). Pass Tesco Superstore on the left and turn into Shaftesbury Avenue near McDonalds. The Arena is a short distance along on the right.

SPENNYMOOR TOWN FC

Founded: 2005 (Formed by the amalgamation of Evenwood Town and the defunct Spennymoor United)
Former Names: None
Nickname: 'The Moors'
Ground: The Brewery Field, Wood Vue, Spennymoor, Co. Durham DL16 6JN
Record Attendance: 7,202 (30th March 1957)
Colours: Black and White striped shirts, Black shorts
Telephone Nº: (01388) 813255
Ground Capacity: 3,000
Seating Capacity: 742
Web Site: www.spennymoortownfc.co.uk

GENERAL INFORMATION

Car Parking: Street parking sometimes available but fans are recommended to use the car parks behind the Town Hall and Leisure Centre or use the old Durham Road School for parking.
Coach Parking: Please contact Steven Lawson on 07871 206474 for information
Nearest Railway Station: Durham (6 miles)
Nearest Bus Station: Durham – the No. 6 bus which stops in Durham Road, Spennymoor (15 minute journey)
Club Shop: At the ground
Opening Times: Matchdays only
Telephone Nº: (01388) 813255

GROUND INFORMATION

Away Supporters' Entrances & Sections:
Turnstile 7 for access to the Ramside Hall Estates Main Stand and the Motif8 Stand when segregation in is place.

ADMISSION INFO (2023/2024 PRICES)

Adult Standing/Seating: £15.00
Over-60s Standing/Seating: £10.00
Under-18s Standing/Seating: £5.00

DISABLED INFORMATION

Wheelchairs: Accommodated by arrangement. Entrance via the Wood Vue turnstiles and Tees Crescent
Helpers: One helper admitted per wheelchair
Prices: Normal prices are charged for fans with disabilities. Helpers are admitted free of charge
Disabled Toilets: 2 available in the ground

Travelling Supporters' Information:
Routes: Exit the A1(M) at Junction 60 and follow the A689 to Rushyford. Take the 3rd exit at the Rushyford roundabout onto the A167 then the 3rd exit at the Chilton roundabout, continuing on the A167 towards Spennymoor. Take the first exit at the Thinford roundabout onto the A688, carry straight on at the small roundabout then take the 3rd exit at the next roundabout into St. Andrew's Lane. Continue along St. Andrew's Lane, turning left at the first roundabout then take the 2nd exit at the mini-roundabout, passing Asda into King Street, and the 2nd exit at the next mini-roundabout into Durham Road. Bear right along Durham Road and Wood Vue is on the left after a short distance.

TAMWORTH FC

Founded: 1933
Former Names: None
Nickname: 'The Lambs'
Ground: The Lamb Ground, Kettlebrook, Tamworth, B77 1AA
Record Attendance: 4,920 (3rd April 1948)

Colours: Red & Black striped shirts with Black shorts
Telephone N°: (01827) 65798
Ground Capacity: 4,118
Seating Capacity: 520
Web site: www.tamworthfc.co.uk

GENERAL INFORMATION

Car Parking: 200 spaces available at the ground – £2.00 per car, £5.00 for per minibus or £10.00 per coach
Coach Parking: At the ground
Nearest Railway Station: Tamworth (½ mile)
Nearest Bus Station: Tamworth (½ mile)
Club Shop: At the ground
Opening Times: Weekdays from 10.00am to 4.00pm and also on Matchdays
Telephone N°: (01827) 65798 Option 3

GROUND INFORMATION

Away Supporters' Entrances & Sections:
Gates 1 and 2 for Terracing, Gate 2A for seating

ADMISSION INFO (2023/2024 PRICES)

Adult Standing: £13.00
Adult Seating: £15.00
Under-18s Standing: £5.00
Under-18s Seating: £7.00
Under-16s Standing: £3.00 (Under-5s free)
Under-16s Seating: £5.00
Under-5s Seating: £2.00
Concessionary Standing: £9.00
Concessionary Seating: £11.00

DISABLED INFORMATION

Wheelchairs: Accommodated
Helpers: Admitted
Prices: Normal prices apply for Wheelchair disabled. Helpers are charged concessionary rates
Disabled Toilets: Yes
Contact: (01827) 65798 (Bookings are advisable)

Travelling Supporters' Information:
Routes: Exit the M42 at Junction 10 and take the A5/A51 to the town centre following signs for Town Centre/Snowdome. Then follow signs for Kettlebrook and the ground is in Kettlebrook Road, 50 yards from the traffic island by the Railway Viaduct and the Snowdome. The ground is signposted from all major roads.

WARRINGTON TOWN FC

Founded: 1949
Former Names: Stockton Heath Albion FC
Nickname: 'The Town'
Ground: Cantilever Park, Loushers Lane, Latchford, Warrington WA4 2RS
Ground Capacity: 2,550 **Seating Capacity**: 500
Record Attendance: 1,400
Colours: Yellow and Blue shirts with Blue shorts
Telephone Nº: (01925) 653044
Web Site: www.warringtontownfc.co.uk

GENERAL INFORMATION

Car Parking: Street parking only
Coach Parking: Street parking only
Nearest Railway Station: Warrington Central (2 miles)
Club Shop: None
Opening Times: –

GROUND INFORMATION

Away Supporters' Entrances & Sections:
No usual segregation

ADMISSION INFO (2023/2024 PRICES)

Adult Standing: £12.00
Adult Seating: £12.00
Senior Citizen Standing: £8.00
Senior Citizen Seating: £8.00
Under-16s Standing/Seating: £3.00

DISABLED INFORMATION

Wheelchairs: Accommodated
Helpers: Admitted
Prices: Normal prices apply for the disabled and helpers
Disabled Toilets: None
Contact: (01925) 653044 (Bookings are not necessary)

Travelling Supporters' Information:
Routes: Exit the M6 at Junction 20 and take the A50 (signposted Warrington/Lymm). Stay on this road (Knutsford Road) and cross the Manchester Ship Canal before turning left into the B5157 Station Road. At the end of the road, turn left into Wash Lane and the ground is immediately ahead.

THE VANARAMA NATIONAL LEAGUE SOUTH

Address

4th Floor, 20 Waterloo Street,
Birmingham B2 5TB

Web site www.thenationalleague.org.uk

Clubs for the 2023/2024 Season

AVELEY FC

Founded: 1927
Former Names: None
Nickname: 'The Millers'
Ground: Parkside, Park Lane, Aveley RM15 4PX
Record Attendance: 3,741 (at Mill Field)

Colours: Royal Blue shirts and shorts
Telephone Nº: 07946438540
Ground Capacity: 3,500
Seating Capacity: 424
Web Site: www.pitchero.com/clubs/aveley

GENERAL INFORMATION

Car Parking: At the ground
Coach Parking: At the ground
Nearest Railway Station: Ockendon (2.9 miles)
Club Shop: At the ground
Opening Times: Matchdays only 2.00pm to 6.00pm

GROUND INFORMATION

Away Supporters' Entrances & Sections:
No usual segregation

ADMISSION INFO (2023/2024 PRICES)

Adult Standing: £15.00
Adult Seating: £15.00
Senior Citizen Standing: £10.00
Senior Citizen Seating: £10.00
Under-16s Standing: £5.00
Under-16s Seating: £5.00

DISABLED INFORMATION

Wheelchairs: Accommodated
Helpers: Admitted
Prices: Normal prices apply for the disabled but helpers are free of charge.
Disabled Toilets: Available
Contact: 07946438540 (Bookings are not necessary)

Travelling Supporters' Information:
Routes: Clockwise on the M25, exit at Jct 30/31 and use the 2nd from left lane to the A13 exit for Thurrock (Lakeside) and at Mar Dyke Interchange take 2nd exit then at roundabout exit into Ship Lane. Continue to next roundabout then take 2nd exit onto High Street and continue into Stifford Rd. At roundabout take 1st exit onto Aveley Bypass (B1335) then at roundabout take 3rd exit merging onto Park Lanr and the ground is on the right.

BATH CITY FC

Founded: 1889
Former Names: Bath AFC, Bath Railway FC and Bath Amateurs FC
Nickname: 'The Romans'
Ground: Twerton Park, Bath BA2 1DB
Record Attendance: 18,020 (1960 vs Brighton & HA)
Colours: Black and White striped shirts, Black shorts
Telephone Nº: (01225) 423087
Ground Capacity: 3,528
Seating Capacity: 1,006
Web site: www.bathcityfc.com
E-mail: info@bathcityfootballclub.co.uk

GENERAL INFORMATION

Car Parking: 93 spaces available at the ground
Coach Parking: Available at the ground (Avon Street)
Nearest Railway Station: Oldfield Park (1 mile)
Nearest Bus Station: Dorchester Street, Bath
Club Shop: At the ground
Opening Times: Matchdays only
Telephone Nº: (01225) 423087

GROUND INFORMATION

Away Supporters' Entrances & Sections:
Turnstiles 17-19 for the Bristol End and Family Stand

ADMISSION INFO (2023/2024 PRICES)

Adult Standing: £16.00 **Adult Seating**: £17.00
Concessionary Standing: £13.00 **Seating**: £14.00
Student Standing: £8.00 **Student Seating**: £9.00
Under-16s Standing: £3.00 **Under-16s Seating**: £5.00

DISABLED INFORMATION

Wheelchairs: 10 spaces available each for home and away fans in front of the Family Stand
Helpers: Admitted
Prices: Concessionary prices are charged to disabled fans. Free for helpers
Disabled Toilets: 2 are available behind the Family Stand
Contact: (01225) 423087 (Bookings are necessary)

Travelling Supporters' Information:
Route: As a recommendation, avoid exiting the M4 at Junction 18 as the road takes you through Bath City Centre. Instead, exit the M4 at Junction 19 onto the M32. Turn off the M32 at Junction 1 and follow the A4174 Bristol Ring Road south then join the A4 for Bath. On the A4, after passing through Saltford you will reach a roundabout shortly before entering Bath. Take the 2nd exit at this roundabout then follow the road before turning left into Newton Road at the bottom of the steep hill. The ground is then on the right hand side of the road.

BRAINTREE TOWN FC

Founded: 1898
Former Names: Manor Works FC, Crittall Athletic FC, Braintree & Crittall Athletic FC and Braintree FC
Nickname: 'The Iron'
Ground: Dunmow Group Stadium, Clockhouse Way, Braintree, Essex CM7 3DE
Record Attendance: 4,000 (May 1952)
Ground Capacity: 4,222
Seating Capacity: 553
Colours: Orange shirts and socks with Blue shorts
Telephone Nº: (01376) 345617
Web site: www.braintreetownfc.org.uk
E-mail: braintreetfc@aol.com

GENERAL INFORMATION

Car Parking: At the ground
Coach Parking: At the ground
Nearest Railway Station: Braintree (1 mile)
Nearest Bus Station: Braintree
Club Shop: At the ground
Opening Times: Matchdays only
Telephone Nº: (01376) 345617

GROUND INFORMATION

Away Supporters' Entrances & Sections:
Gates 7-8 for accommodation in the Quag End

ADMISSION INFO (2023/2024 PRICES)

Adult Standing/Seating: £15.00
Concessionary Standing/Seating: £10.00
Under-18s Standing: £5.00

DISABLED INFORMATION

Wheelchairs: Accommodated – 6 spaces available in the Main Stand
Helpers: Admitted
Prices: Normal prices apply for fans with disabilities. Helpers are admitted free of charge
Disabled Toilets: Available
Contact: (01376) 345617

Travelling Supporters' Information:
Routes: Exit the A120 Braintree Bypass at the McDonald's roundabout and follow Cressing Road northwards. The floodlights at the ground are visible on the left ½ mile into town. Turn left into Clockhouse Way then left again for the ground.

CHELMSFORD CITY FC

Founded: 1938
Former Names: Chelmsford FC
Nickname: 'City' or 'Clarets'
Ground: Melbourne Community Stadium, Salerno Way, Chelmsford CM1 2EH
Record Attendance: 16,807 (at New Writtle Street)
Colours: Claret and White shirts and shorts
Telephone Nº: (01245) 290959
Ground Capacity: 3,000
Seating Capacity: 1,400
Web site: www.chelmsfordcityfc.com
E-mail: info@chelmsfordcityfc.com

GENERAL INFORMATION

Car Parking: Limited space at ground and street parking
Coach Parking: Two spaces available at the ground subject to advance notice
Nearest Railway Station: Chelmsford (2 miles)
Nearest Bus Station: Chelmsford (2 miles)
Club Shop: At the ground
Opening Times: Matchdays only
Telephone Nº: (01245) 290959

GROUND INFORMATION

Away Supporters' Entrances & Sections:
No usual segregation

ADMISSION INFO (2023/2024 PRICES)

Adult Standing/Seating: £17.50
17s - 24s (with Student ID) & 12s - 16s £7.00
Under-12s (with paying Adult): Free of charge
Concessionary Standing/Seating: £12.50
Note: Tickets are cheaper when purchased online

DISABLED INFORMATION

Wheelchairs: Spaces for 11 wheelchairs available
Helpers: Admitted free of charge
Prices: Normal prices apply for fans with disabilities
Disabled Toilets: Available
Contact: (01245) 290959 (Bookings are necessary)

Travelling Supporters' Information:
Route: The ground is situated next to the only set of high rise flats in Chelmsford which can therefore be used as a landmark. From the A12 from London: Exit the A12 at Junction 15 signposted for Chelmsford/Harlow/A414 and head towards Chelmsford along the dual-carriageway. At the third roundabout, immediately after passing the 'Superbowl' on the left, take the first exit into Westway, signposted for the Crematorium and Widford Industrial Estate. Continue along Westway which becomes Waterhouse Lane after the second set of traffic lights. At the next set of lights (at the gyratory system) take the first exit into Rainsford Road, signposted for Sawbridgeworth A1060. Continue along Rainsford Road then turn right into Chignal Road at the second set of traffic lights. Turn right again into Melbourne Avenue and Salerno Way is on the left at the end of the football pitches.

CHIPPENHAM TOWN FC

Founded: 1873
Former Names: None
Nickname: 'The Bluebirds'
Ground: The Thornbury Surfacing Stadium, Hardenhuish Park, Bristol Road, Chippenham, Wiltshire SN14 6LR
Record Attendance: 4,800 (1951)

Colours: Blue shirts, shorts and socks
Telephone Nº: (01249) 650400
Ground Capacity: 3,000
Seating Capacity: 300
Web site: www.chippenhamtown.com

GENERAL INFORMATION

Car Parking: Adjacent to the ground
Coach Parking: At the ground
Nearest Railway Station: Chippenham (1 mile)
Nearest Bus Station: Chippenham
Club Shop: At the ground
Opening Times: Matchdays only
Telephone Nº: (01249) 650400

GROUND INFORMATION

Away Supporters' Entrances & Sections:
No usual segregation

ADMISSION INFO (2023/2024 PRICES)

Adult Standing: £15.00
Adult Seating: £15.00
Concessionary/Student Standing: £11.00
Concessionary/Student Seating: £11.00
Under-18s Standing/Seating: £3.00
Note: Under-16s are admitted free of charge when accompanied by a paying adult.

DISABLED INFORMATION

Wheelchairs: Accommodated at front of Stand
Helpers: Admitted
Prices: Normal prices apply for fans with disabilities. Helpers are admitted free of charge.
Disabled Toilets: Available in the Clubhouse
Contact: (01249) 650400 (Bookings are not necessary)

Travelling Supporters' Information:
Routes: Exit the M4 at Junction 17 and take the A350. Turn right at the first roundabout and follow the road to the junction with the A420. Turn left following 'Town Centre' signs and the ground is just over ½ mile on the left near the Pelican crossing.

DARTFORD FC

Founded: 1888
Former Names: None
Nickname: 'The Darts'
Ground: Princes Park Stadium, Grassbanks, Darenth Road, Dartford DA1 1RT
Record Attendance: 4,097 (11th November 2006)

Colours: White Shirts with Black Shorts
Telephone Nº: (01322) 299991
Ground Capacity: 4,118
Seating Capacity: 640
Web Site: www.dartfordfc.com
E-mail: info@dartfordfc.com

GENERAL INFORMATION

Car Parking: At the ground
Coach Parking: At the ground
Nearest Railway Station: Dartford (½ mile)
Nearest Bus Station: Dartford (½ mile) & Bluewater (2 miles)
Club Shop: At the ground plus online sales
Opening Times: Matchdays only – 1.00pm to 6.00pm (but the stadium itself is open daily).
Telephone Nº: (01322) 299991

ADMISSION INFO (2023/2024 PRICES)

Adult Standing: £15.00
Adult Seating: £15.00
Senior Citizen/Concessionary Standing: £10.00
Senior Citizen/Concessionary Seating: £10.00
Youth (Ages 13 to 17) Standing/Seating: £5.00
Junior (Ages 5 to 12) Standing/Seating: £2.00
Under-5s Standing/Seating: Free of charge

DISABLED INFORMATION

Wheelchairs: 9 spaces available in total around the ground
Helpers: Admitted
Prices: Normal prices for the disabled. Free for helpers
Disabled Toilets: Available behind each goal, in the main reception and on the upper floor.
Contact: (01322) 299991 (Bookings are not necessary)

Travelling Supporters' Information:
Routes: From M25 Clockwise: Exit the M25 at Junction 1B. At the roundabout, take the 3rd exit onto Princes Road (A225) then the second exit at the next roundabout.* Continue downhill to the traffic lights (with the ground on the left), turn left into Darenth Road then take the 2nd left for the Car Park; From M25 Anti-clockwise: Exit the M25 at Junction 2 and follow the A225 to the roundabout. Take the first exit at this roundabout then the 2nd exit at the next roundabout. Then as from * above.

DOVER ATHLETIC FC

Founded: 1983
Former Names: None
Nickname: 'The Whites'
Ground: Crabble Athletic Ground, Lewisham Road, River, Dover CT17 0JB
Record Attendance: 7,000 (vs Folkestone in 1951)
Colours: White shirts with Black shorts
Telephone Nº: (01304) 822373
Ground Capacity: 5,745
Seating Capacity: 1,500
Web site: www.doverathletic.com
E-mail: enquiries@doverathletic.com

GENERAL INFORMATION

Car Parking: Street parking
Coach Parking: Street parking
Nearest Railway Station: Kearsney (1 mile)
Nearest Bus Station: Pencester Road, Dover (1½ miles)
Club Shop: At the ground
Opening Times: Saturdays 9.00am to 12.00pm
Telephone Nº: (01304) 822373

GROUND INFORMATION

Away Supporters' Entrances & Sections:
Segregation only used when required

ADMISSION INFO (2023/2024 PRICES)

Adult Standing/Seating: £17.00
Concessionary Standing/Seating: £15.00
Under 18s Standing/Seating: £9.00

DISABLED INFORMATION

Wheelchairs: Approximately 6 spaces are available in the Family Stand
Helpers: Admitted
Prices: Normal prices are applied for the disabled, helpers are admitted free of charge.
Disabled Toilets: Three available
Contact: (01304) 822373 (Bookings are not necessary)

Travelling Supporters' Information:
Routes: Take the A2 to the Whitfield roundabout and take the 4th exit. Travel down the hill to the mini-roundabout then turn left and follow the road for 1 mile to the traffic lights on the hill. Turn sharp right and pass under the railway bridge – the ground is on the left after 300 yards.

EASTBOURNE BOROUGH FC

Founded: 1963
Former Names: Langney Sports FC
Nickname: 'The Sports'
Ground: Langney Sports Club, Priory Lane, Langney, Eastbourne BN23 7QH
Record Attendance: 3,770 (5th November 2005)

Colours: Red and Black shirts with Red shorts
Telephone Nº: (01323) 766265
Ground Capacity: 4,151
Seating Capacity: 542
Web site: www.ebfc.co.uk
E-mail: info@ebfc.co.uk

GENERAL INFORMATION

Car Parking: Around 400 spaces available at the ground
Coach Parking: At the ground
Nearest Railway Station: Eastbourne (3 miles)
Nearest Bus Station: Eastbourne (Service 6A to ground)
Club Shop: At the ground
Opening Times: Matchdays only
Telephone Nº: (01323) 766265

GROUND INFORMATION

Away Supporters' Entrances & Sections:
No usual segregation

ADMISSION INFO (2023/2024 PRICES)

Adult Standing: £18.00
Adult Seating: £18.00
Concessionary Standing/Seating: £12.00
Students/Under-12s Standing/Seating: £6.00
Note: Prices are lower for advanced online bookings.

DISABLED INFORMATION

Wheelchairs: 6 spaces available
Helpers: Admitted
Prices: Normal prices apply for fans with disabilities. Free of charge for helpers
Disabled Toilets: Available
Contact: (01323) 766265 (Bookings are necessary)

Travelling Supporters' Information:
Routes: From the North: Exit the A22 onto the Polegate bypass, signposted A27 Eastbourne, Hastings & Bexhill. *Take the 2nd exit at the next roundabout for Stone Cross and Westham (A22) then the first exit at the following roundabout signposted Stone Cross and Westham. Turn right after ½ mile into Friday Street (B2104). At the end of Friday Street, turn left at the double mini-roundabout into Hide Hollow (B2191), passing Eastbourne Crematorium on your right. Turn right at the roundabout into Priory Road, and Priory Lane is about 200 yards down the road on the left; Approaching on the A27 from Brighton: Turn left at the Polegate traffic lights then take 2nd exit at the large roundabout to join the bypass. Then as from *.

FARNBOROUGH FC

Founded: 1967 (Re-formed in 2007)
Former Names: Farnborough Town FC
Nickname: 'The Boro'
Ground: Easy as HGV Stadium, Cherrywood Road, Farnborough GU14 8UD
Record Attendance: 4,267 (15th May 2011)

Colours: Yellow and Blue shirts and shorts
Telephone Nº: 07503683370
Ground Capacity: 4,190
Seating Capacity: 3,135
Web site: www.farnboroughfc.co.uk
E-mail contact: info@farnboroughfc.co.uk

GENERAL INFORMATION

Car Parking: 260 spaces available at the ground with a further 200 spaces at the nearby Sixth Form college
Coach Parking: At the ground
Nearest Railway Stations: Farnborough (Main), Farnborough North, Frimley and Blackwater
Nearest Bus Station: Buses from Farnborough Main stop just outside the ground – please check the web site for details.
Club Shop: At the ground + web sales in the near future
Opening Times: Matchdays only

GROUND INFORMATION

Away Supporters' Entrances & Sections:
Moor Road entrances and accommodation

ADMISSION INFO (2023/2024 PRICES)

Adult Standing: £15.00
Adult Seating (Platinum Lounge): £19.00
Concessionary Standing: £10.00
Concessionary Seating: £10.00
14s-16s : £5.00
Under-14s : Free of charge with a paying Adult
Note: In keeping with F.A. Regulations, the Club reserves the right to charge higher prices for F.A. Trophy and F.A. Cup games.

DISABLED INFORMATION

Wheelchairs: Spaces available in a disabled section in the PRE Stand
Helpers: Admitted free of charge
Prices: Normal prices charged for disabled fans
Disabled Toilets: Available in the PRE Stand
Contact: 07950394150 (Bookings are necessary)

Travelling Supporters' Information:
Routes: Exit the M3 at Junction 4 and take the A331 signposted for Farnham. After a few hundred yards exit at the second slip road – signposted A325 Farnborough – turn right at the roundabout and cross over the dual carriageway and a small roundabout. Pass the Farnborough Gate shopping centre on your left and at the next roundabout turn left onto the A325. Go over a pelican crossing and at the next set of lights take the right filter lane into Prospect Avenue. At the end of this road turn right at the roundabout into Cherrywood Road. The ground is on the right after ½ mile.

HAMPTON & RICHMOND BOROUGH FC

Founded: 1921
Former Names: Hampton FC
Nickname: 'Beavers'
Ground: The Beveree Stadium, Beaver Close, off Station Road, Hampton, Middlesex TW12 2BX
Record Attendance: 3,225 (vs AFC Wimbledon, 2009)
Colours: Blue and Red Striped shirts with Red shorts
Matchday Phone Nº: (020) 8979-2456
Ground Capacity: 3,500
Seating Capacity: 644
Web site: www.hamptonfc.net

GENERAL INFORMATION

Car Parking: At the ground and street parking
Coach Parking: Contact the Club for information
Nearest Railway Station: Hampton
Nearest Bus Station: Hounslow/Kingston/Fulwell
Club Shop: At the ground
Opening Times: Matchdays only
Telephone Nº: (020) 8979-2456

GROUND INFORMATION

Away Supporters' Entrances & Sections:
No usual segregation

ADMISSION INFO (2023/2024 PRICES)

Adult Standing: £15.00
Adult Seating: £15.00
Senior Citizen/Concessionary Standing: £11.00
Senior Citizen/Concessionary Seating: £11.00
Youths 13s-17s Standing/Seating: £5.00
Juniors 5s-12s Standing/Seating: £3.00
Note: Under-5s are admitted free of charge with an Adult

DISABLED INFORMATION

Wheelchairs: Accommodated in front of the main stand
Helpers: Admitted
Prices: Normal prices apply
Disabled Toilets: Available
Contact: (020) 8979-2456 (Bookings are not necessary)

Travelling Supporters' Information:
Routes: From the South: Exit the M3 at Junction 1 and follow the A308 (signposted Kingston). Turn 1st left after Kempton Park into Percy Road. Turn right at the level crossing into Station Road then left into Beaver Close for the ground; From the North: Take the A305 from Twickenham then turn left onto the A311. Pass through Hampton Hill onto Hampton High Street. Turn right at the White Hart pub (just before the junction with the A308), then right into Station Road and right again into Beaver Close.

HAVANT & WATERLOOVILLE FC

Founded: 1998
Former Names: Formed by the amalgamation of Waterlooville FC and Havant Town FC
Nickname: 'The Hawks'
Ground: Westleigh Park, Martin Road, Havant, PO9 5TH
Record Attendance: 4,400 (2006/07)

Colours: White shirts and shorts
Telephone Nº: (023) 9278-7822 (Ground)
Ground Capacity: 5,300
Seating Capacity: 710
Web site: www.havantandwaterloovillefc.co.uk
E-mail: generalmanager@havantandwaterloovillefc.co.uk

GENERAL INFORMATION

Car Parking: Space for 300 cars at the ground
Coach Parking: At the ground
Nearest Railway Station: Havant (1 mile)
Nearest Bus Station: Town Centre (1½ miles)
Club Shop: At the ground
Opening Times: Matchdays only
Telephone Nº: 07768 271143

GROUND INFORMATION

Away Supporters' Entrances & Sections:
No usual segregation

ADMISSION INFO (2023/2024 PRICES)

Adult Standing: £15.00
Adult Seating: £15.00
Concessionary Standing/Seating: £10.00
Students Standing/Seating: £10.00
Note: When accompanied by a paying adult, children under the age of 16 are admitted free of charge

DISABLED INFORMATION

Wheelchairs: 12 spaces available in the Main Stand
Helpers: Admitted
Prices: Normal prices for disabled fans. Free for helpers
Disabled Toilets: Two available
Contact: (023) 9226-7822 (Bookings are necessary)

Travelling Supporters' Information:
Routes: From London or the North take the A27 from Chichester and exit at the B2149 turn-off for Havant. Take the 2nd exit off the dual carriageway into Bartons Road and then the 1st right into Martin Road for the ground; From the West: Take the M27 then the A27 to the Petersfield exit. Then as above.

HEMEL HEMPSTEAD TOWN FC

Founded: 1885
Former Names: Apsley FC and Hemel Hempstead FC
Nickname: 'The Tudors'
Ground: Vauxhall Road, Adeyfield, Hemel Hempstead HP2 4HW
Record Attendance: 2,840 (vs Gosport Borough 6th May 2013)
Colours: Shirts and Shorts are Red with White trim
Telephone Nº: (01442) 251521
Ground Capacity: 3,152
Seating Capacity: 534
Web site: www.hemelfc.com
E-mail: info@hemelfc.com

GENERAL INFORMATION

Car Parking: At the ground
Coach Parking: At the ground
Nearest Railway Station: Hemel Hempstead (1½ miles)
Nearest Bus Station: Hemel Hempstead (¾ mile)
Club Shop: At the ground
Opening Times: Matchdays only

GROUND INFORMATION

Away Supporters' Entrances & Sections:
No usual segregation

ADMISSION INFO (2023/2024 PRICES)

Adult Standing/Seating: £15.00
Concessionary Standing/Seating: £10.00
Students Standing/Seating: £10.00
NHS Workers/ Armed Forces: £8.00
Note: Under-16s are admitted for free with a paying adult

DISABLED INFORMATION

Wheelchairs: Accommodated
Helpers: Admitted
Prices: Normal prices for disabled. Helpers are admitted free
Disabled Toilets: Available in the Clubhouse
Contact: via Email

Travelling Supporters' Information:
Routes: Exit the M1 at Junction 8 and go straight ahead at the first roundabout. When approaching the 2nd roundabout move into the right hand lane and, as you continue straight across be ready to turn right almost immediately through a gap in the central reservation. This turn-off is Leverstock Green Road and continue along this to the double mini-roundabout. At this roundabout turn left into Vauxhall Road and the ground is on the right at the next roundabout.

MAIDSTONE UNITED FC

Founded: 1992 (Reformed)
Former Names: Maidstone Invicta FC
Nickname: 'The Stones'
Ground: Gallagher Stadium, James Whatman Way, Maidstone ME14 1LQ
Record Attendance: 4,101 (15th July 2017)

Colours: Amber shirts with Black shorts
Telephone Nº: (01622) 753817
Ground Capacity: 4,191
Seating Capacity: 750
Web Site: www.maidstoneunited.co.uk
E-mail: itucker@maidstoneunited.co.uk

GENERAL INFORMATION

Car Parking: Various Pay & Display Car Parks available near the ground
Coach Parking: Maidstone coach park (1¼ miles) – please contact the club for further information
Nearest Railway Station: Maidstone East (¼ mile)
Club Shop: Available at the ground
Opening Times: Saturday Matchdays 12.30pm to 5.00pm; Tuesday Matchdays 6.15pm to 9.30pm.
Telephone Nº: (01622) 753817

GROUND INFORMATION

Away Supporters' Entrances & Sections:
No usual segregation – use the main turnstiles unless otherwise advertised. If segregation is in force, visiting fans should use turnstile 8 for accommodation in the North East Corner.

ADMISSION INFO (2023/2024 PRICES)

Adult Standing: £17.00
Adult Seating: £20.00
Senior Citizen/Student Standing: £13.00
Senior Citizen/Student Seating: £16.00
Ages 11 to 16 Standing: £7.00
Ages 11 to 16 Seating: £10.00
Under-11s Standing: Free with paying Adult
Under-11s Seating: £3.00

DISABLED INFORMATION

Wheelchairs: Accommodated in the Manchett Main Stand and Genco Stand. The latter has 2 spaces for wheelchairs of away fans.
Helpers: Admitted
Prices: Normal prices apply for the disabled. Free for helpers
Disabled Toilets: Available
Contact: (01622) 753817 (Bookings are essential)

Travelling Supporters' Information:
Routes: Exit the M20 at Junction 6 or the M2 at Junction 3 and follow the A229 into Maidstone. After entering Maidstone, at the second roundabout (by the White Rabbit pub), take the third exit into James Whatman Way for the stadium. Please check the club web site for details of the nearest car parks.

SLOUGH TOWN FC

Image courtesy of Gary House Photography

Founded: 1890
Former Names: Slough FC and Slough United FC
Nickname: 'The Rebels'
Ground: Arbour Park, Stoke Road, Slough SL2 5AY
Record Attendance: 1,950 (vs Rochdale, 4/12/2017)
Contact Telephone Nº: 07792 126124

Colours: Shirts are Amber with Navy Blue sleeves, shorts are Navy Blue
Ground Capacity: 2,000
Seating Capacity: 548
Web site: www.sloughtownfc.net
E-mail: gensec@sloughtownfc.net

GENERAL INFORMATION

Car Parking: At the ground, at St. Joseph's Catholic High School and in other local car parks
Coach Parking: At the ground
Nearest Railway Station: Slough (¾ mile)
Nearest Bus Station: Slough (¾ mile)
Club Shop: At the ground
Opening Times: Matchdays only
Telephone Nº: 07933 221337 (Sue Shiel)

GROUND INFORMATION

Away Supporters' Entrances & Sections:
No usual segregation

ADMISSION INFO (2023/2024 PRICES)

Adult Standing/Seating: £15.00 (£13.00 online)
Concessions Standing/Seating: £10.00 (£8.00 online)
14s-17s Standing/Seating: £5.00 (£3.00 online)
Under-14s Standing/Seating: £1.00
Note: Under-12s must be accompanied by an adult.

DISABLED INFORMATION

Wheelchairs: Accommodated (enter via the front entrance)
Helpers: Admitted. A free carers pass is available. Download the relevant form from the club's web site.
Prices: Normal prices apply for the disabled and helpers
Disabled Toilets: Available
Contact: 07792 126124 (Bookings are not necessary) – E-mail: gensec@sloughtownfc.net

Travelling Supporters' Information:
Routes: From the South: Exit the M4 at Junction 5 and head west on the A4 (London Road) for approximately 2¾ miles. Pass the Tesco Extra store and the turning to Slough Railway station on your right then turn right onto Stoke Road (B416). Continue along Stoke Road for ¾ mile then Arbour Park is on the right; From the North: Exit the M40 at Junction 2 and head south on the A355 towards Slough. After approximately 1½ miles, turn left onto Parish Lane by the Indian Courtyard and at the end of the road, turn right onto Windsor Road (B416). After 2 miles take the second exit at the roundabout, continuing on the B416 and Arbour Park is on the left after approximately 1 mile.

ST. ALBANS CITY FC

Founded: 1908
Former Names: None
Nickname: 'The Saints'
Ground: Mozzarella Fellas Stadium, Clarence Park, York Road, St. Albans, AL1 4PL
Record Attendance: 9,757 (27th February 1926)

Colours: Yellow shirts with Blue trim, Blue shorts
Telephone Nº: (01727) 848914
Ground Capacity: 5,007
Seating Capacity: 667
Web site: www.stalbanscityfc.com
E-mail: Contact the club via the form on the website

GENERAL INFORMATION

Car Parking: Street parking or in the railway station car park (£2.50 charge)
Coach Parking: In Clarence Park
Nearest Railway Station: St. Albans City (200 yds)
Club Shop: At the ground
Opening Times: Matchdays only
Telephone Nº: (01727) 848914

GROUND INFORMATION

Away Supporters' Entrances & Sections:
No usual segregation but the South Stand can be used for away fans if necessary.

ADMISSION INFO (2023/2024 PRICES)

Adult Standing/Seating: £16.50
Concessionary Standing/Seating: £11.00
18s - 23s Standing/Seating: £8.00
Under-18s Standing/Seating: £6.00
Note: Under-12s are admitted free of charge when accompanied by a paying adult

DISABLED INFORMATION

Wheelchairs: Accommodated
Helpers: One admitted per disabled supporter
Prices: Normal prices for the disabled. Helpers free of charge
Disabled Toilets: Available in the York Road End
Contact: (01727) 848914 (Bookings are not necessary)

Travelling Supporters' Information:
Routes: Take the M1 or M10 to the A405 North Orbital Road and at the roundabout at the start of the M10, go north on the A5183 (Watling Street). Turn right along St. Stephen's Hill and carry along into St. Albans. Continue up Holywell Hill, go through two sets of traffic lights and at the end of St. Peter's Street, take a right turn at the roundabout into Hatfield Road. Follow over the mini-roundabouts and at the second set of traffic lights turn left into Clarence Road and the ground is on the left. Park in Clarence Road and enter the ground via the Park or in York Road and use the entrance by the footbridge.

TAUNTON TOWN FC

Founded: 1947
Former Names: None
Nickname: 'The Peacocks'
Ground: Wordsworth Drive, Taunton TA1 2HG
Record Attendance: 3,284 (1999)

Colours: Sky Blue shirts with Claret shorts
Telephone Nº: (01823) 254909
Ground Capacity: 2,500
Seating Capacity: 300
Web Site: www.tauntontown.com
E-mail: admin@tauntontown.com

GENERAL INFORMATION

Car Parking: At the ground
Coach Parking: At the ground
Nearest Railway Station: Taunton (1¼ miles)
Club Shop: None

GROUND INFORMATION

Away Supporters' Entrances & Sections:
No usual segregation

ADMISSION INFO (2023/2024 PRICES)

Adult Standing/Seating: £14.00
Concessions Standing/Seating: £1.00
Ages 13 to 18 Standing/Seating: £5.00
Ages 6 to 12 Standing/Seating: £2.00
Under-6s are admitted free with paying Adult

DISABLED INFORMATION

Wheelchairs: Accommodated
Helpers: Admitted
Prices: Normal prices apply for the disabled. Helpers pay concessionary prices
Disabled Toilets: Available
Contact: (01823) 254909 (Bookings are not necessary)

Travelling Supporters' Information:
Routes: Exit the M5 at Junction 25 and follow signs for Taunton Town Centre. Bear left at the first set of traffic lights then go straight on at the next set of traffic lights into Wordsworth Drive. The ground is on the left hand side of the road after approximately 200 yards.

TONBRIDGE ANGELS FC

Founded: 1948
Former Names: Tonbridge FC
Nickname: 'The Angels'
Ground: The Halcyon Wealth Longmead Stadium, Darenth Avenue, Tonbridge TN10 3JF
Record Attendance: 2,411 (7th May 2011)

Colours: Blue and White shirts with White shorts
Telephone Nº: (01732) 352417
Ground Capacity: 3,014
Seating Capacity: 774
Web site: www.tonbridgeangels.co.uk
E-mail: charlie.cole@tonbridgeangels.co.uk

GENERAL INFORMATION

Car Parking: At the ground
Coach Parking: At the ground
Nearest Railway Station: Tonbridge (2 miles)
Club Shop: At the ground
Opening Times: Matchdays only plus online sales
Telephone Nº: (01732) 352417

GROUND INFORMATION

Away Supporters' Entrances & Sections:
No usual segregation

ADMISSION INFO (2023/2024 PRICES)

Adult Standing: £16.00
Adult Seating: £17.00
Senior Citizen Standing: £13.00
Senior Citizen Seating: £14.00
12s - 17s Standing: £7.00
Under-12s : Free with a paying Adult
Under-15s Must be accompanied by an Adult

DISABLED INFORMATION

Wheelchairs: Accommodated
Helpers: Admitted
Prices: Normal prices apply
Disabled Toilets: One available
Contact: (01732) 352417

Travelling Supporters' Information:
Routes: Take the A26 or A21 to Tonbridge Town Centre, pass through the High Street and head north up Shipbourne Road which is the A227 Gravesend road. Turn left at the 2nd mini-roundabout by the 'Pinnacles' Pub into Darenth Avenue. The ground is situated at the bottom end of Darenth Avenue.

TORQUAY UNITED FC

Founded: 1899
Former Name: Torquay Town FC (1899-1910)
Nickname: 'Gulls'
Ground: Plainmoor Ground, Torquay TQ1 3PS
Ground Capacity: 6,200
Seating Capacity: 2,841
Record Attendance: 21,908 (29th January 1955)

Colours: Yellow shirts and Blue shorts
Telephone Nº: (01803) 328666
Ticket Office: (01803) 328666
Web Site: www.torquayunited.com
E-mail: reception@torquayunited.com

GENERAL INFORMATION

Car Parking: Street parking
Coach Parking: Lymington Road Coach Station (½ mile)
Nearest Railway Station: Torre (1¼ miles) or Torquay (2 miles)
Nearest Bus Station: Lymington Road (½ mile)
Club Shop: At the ground
Opening Times: Monday to Friday 10.00am to 4.30pm, Tuesday Matchdays 10.00am until kick-off then until after the final whistle until 10.00pm. Saturday Matchdays 12.00pm to 3.00pm then until 5.30pm following the final whistle.
Telephone Nº: (01803) 328666

GROUND INFORMATION

Away Supporters' Entrances & Sections:
Riviera Rentals away terrace

ADMISSION INFO (2023/2024 PRICES)

Adult Standing: £20.00
Adult Seating: £21.00 – £22.00
Concessionary Standing: £18.00
Concessionary Seating: £19.00 – £20.00
Under-18s Standing/Seating: £13.00
Note: Under-7s are admitted free with a paying adult and tickets booked in advance are cheaper.

DISABLED INFORMATION

Wheelchairs: Spaces for both Home and Away fans are available in front of Bristow Bench Stand.
Helpers: One helper admitted per wheelchair
Prices: Normal prices for the disabled. Free for helpers
Disabled Toilets: In the Ellacombe End and the Away End
Contact: (01803) 328666 (Bookings are not necessary)
Jo Harris (Liaison Officer) – joanneh@torquayunited.com

Travelling Supporters' Information:
Routes: From the North and East: Take the M5 to the A38 then A380 to Torquay. On entering Torquay, turn left at the 1st set of traffic lights after Riviera Way Retail Park into Hele Road. Following signs for the ground, continue straight on over two mini-roundabouts, go up West Hill Road to the traffic lights, then straight ahead into Warbro Road. The ground is situated on the right after 200 yards.

TRURO CITY FC

Note: Truro City FC are groundsharing with Plymouth Parkway FC for the 2023/2024 season.
A new stadium in Truro is currently under construction.

Founded: 1889
Former Names: None
Nickname: 'White Tigers'
Ground: Bolitho Park, St. Peter's Road, Manadon, Plymouth PL5 3JH
Record Attendance: N/A

Colours: All White shirts and shorts
Telephone Nº: 07967807432
Ground Capacity: 3,500
Seating Capacity: 250
Web Site: www.trurocityfc.net

GENERAL INFORMATION

Car Parking: Limited parking at the ground
Coach Parking: At the ground
Nearest Railway Station: Plymouth
Club Shop: None

GROUND INFORMATION

Away Supporters' Entrances & Sections:
No usual segregation

ADMISSION INFO (2023/2024 PRICES)

Adult Standing/Seating: £10.00
Concessionary Standing/Seating: £8.00
Under-18s and Students Standing/Seating: £8.00
Note: Under-10s are admitted free with a paying adult and Students should possess ID.
While the club groundshare with Plymouth Parkway FC, buses for their supporters will depart from Truro and details can be found on the club website.

DISABLED INFORMATION

Wheelchairs: Accommodated
Helpers: Admitted
Prices: Normal prices apply for the disabled and helpers
Disabled Toilets: Available
Contact: (07967807432) (Bookings are recommended)

Travelling Supporters' Information:
Routes: Exit the A38 Devon Expressway Plymouth at the Manadon (A386) turn-off and follow St. Peter's Road past Manadon Vale Primary School on the right. Continue along St. Peter's Road for approximately 1 mile and Bolitho Park is situated on the right near the junction with Shakespeare Road.

WELLING UNITED FC

Founded: 1963
Former Names: None
Nickname: 'The Wings'
Ground: Park View Road, Welling, Kent DA16 1SY
Record Attendance: 4,100 (vs Gillingham, 1989)
Colours: Shirts are Red with White trim, Red shorts
Telephone Nº: (0208) 301-1196
Ground Capacity: 4,500
Seating Capacity: 1,000
Web site: www.wellingunited.com

GENERAL INFORMATION

Car Parking: Street parking only
Coach Parking: Outside of the ground
Nearest Railway Station: Welling (¾ mile)
Nearest Bus Station: Bexleyheath
Club Shop: At the ground
Opening Times: Matchdays only
Telephone Nº: (0208) 301-1196

GROUND INFORMATION

Away Supporters' Entrances & Sections:
Accommodation in the Danson Park End and the East Stand

ADMISSION INFO (2023/2024 PRICES)

Adult Standing: £15.00
Adult Seating: £17.00
Concessionary Standing: £10.00
Concessionary Seating: £12.00
Students Standing: £10.00
Students Seating: £12.00
Under-16s Standing: £7.00
Under-11s: Free with a paying adult

DISABLED INFORMATION

Wheelchairs: Accommodated at the side of the Main Stand
Helpers: Admitted
Prices: Concessionary prices for fans with disabilities. Helpers are admitted free of charge
Disabled Toilets: Yes
Contact: (0208) 301-1196 (Bookings are not necessary)

Travelling Supporters' Information:
Routes: Take the A2 (Rochester Way) from London, then the A221 Northwards (Danson Road) to Bexleyheath. At the end turn left towards Welling along Park View Road and the ground is on the left.

WESTON-SUPER-MARE AFC

Founded: 1899
Former Names: Christ Church Old Boys FC
Nickname: 'Seagulls'
Ground: Optima Stadium, Winterstoke Road, Weston-super-Mare BS24 9AA
Record Attendance: 2,949 (vs Doncaster Rov., 2014)

Colours: White shirts with Black shorts
Telephone Nº: (01934) 621618
Ground Capacity: 3,500
Seating Capacity: 500
Web site: www.westonsmareafc.co.uk
E-mail: enquiries@wsmafc.co.uk

GENERAL INFORMATION

Car Parking: 140 spaces available at the ground
Coach Parking: At the ground
Nearest Railway Station: Weston-super-Mare (1½ miles)
Nearest Bus Station: Weston-super-Mare (1½ miles)
Club Shop: At the ground
Opening Times: Matchdays only
Telephone Nº: (01934) 621618

GROUND INFORMATION

Away Supporters' Entrances & Sections:
No usual segregation

ADMISSION INFO (2023/2024 PRICES)

Adult Standing/Seating: £14.00
Concessionary Standing/Seating: £10.00
Students and Under-16s Standing/Seating: £4.50
Note: Under-8s are admitted free of charge when accompanied by a paying adult or senior citizen and Family Tickets are also available.

DISABLED INFORMATION

Wheelchairs: Accommodated in a special disabled section
Helpers: Admitted
Prices: Normal prices apply
Disabled Toilets: Two available
Contact: (01934) 621618 (Bookings are not necessary)

Travelling Supporters' Information:
Routes: Exit the M5 at Junction 21 and follow the dual carriageway (A370) to the 4th roundabout (Asda Winterstoke). Turn left, go over the mini-roundabout and continue for 800 yards. The ground is on the right.

WEYMOUTH FC

Founded: 1890
Former Names: None
Nickname: 'Terras'
Ground: Bob Lucas Stadium, Radipole Lane, Weymouth, Dorset DT4 9XJ
Ground Capacity: 6,600
Seating Capacity: 900

Record Attendance: 6,500 (14th November 2005)
Colours: Sky Blue shirts with Claret trim, Blue shorts
Telephone Nº: (01305) 785558
Web site: www.theterras.co.uk
E-mail: office@weymouthfootballclub.co.uk

GENERAL INFORMATION

Car Parking: 200 spaces available at the ground
Coach Parking: At the ground
Nearest Railway Station: Weymouth (2 miles)
Nearest Bus Station: Weymouth Town Centre
Club Shop: At the ground
Opening Times: Matchdays only
Telephone Nº: (01305) 785558

GROUND INFORMATION

Away Supporters' Entrances & Sections:
No usual segregation

ADMISSION INFO (2023/2024 PRICES)

Adult Standing/Seating: £16.00
Concessionary Standing/Seating: £12.00
13s to 17s Standing/Seating: £6.00
7s to 12s Standing/Seating: £4.00
Under-7s Standing/Seating: free with paying Adult

DISABLED INFORMATION

Wheelchairs: Accommodated pitchside in front of the Main Stand
Helpers: Admitted
Prices: Concessionary prices apply for the disabled. Helpers are admitted free of charge
Disabled Toilets: Available adjacent to the wheelchair area
Contact: (01305) 785558 (Bookings are not necessary)

Travelling Supporters' Information:
Routes: Take the A354 from Dorchester to Weymouth and turn right at the first roundabout to the town centre. Take the 3rd exit at the next roundabout and follow signs for the ground which is about ½ mile on the right.

WORTHING FC

Founded: 1886
Former Names: Worthing Association FC
Nickname: 'The Rebels'
Ground: Woodside Road Stadium, Woodside Road, Worthing BN14 7HQ
Record Attendance: 3,600 (1936)

Colours: Red shirts and shorts
Telephone N°: (01903) 239575
Ground Capacity: 3,650
Seating Capacity: 500
Web site: www.worthingfc.com

GENERAL INFORMATION

Car Parking: Street parking only
Coach Parking: Street parking only
Nearest Railway Station: Worthing Central (½ mile)
Nearest Bus Station: Worthing
Club Shop: At the ground
Opening Times: Matchdays only
Telephone N°: (01903) 239575

GROUND INFORMATION

Away Supporters' Entrances & Sections:
No usual segregation

ADMISSION INFO (2023/2024 PRICES)

Adult Standing/Seating: £16.00
Senior Citizen Standing/Seating: £11.00
Under-16s Standing/Seating: Free with paying Adult (£5.00 otherwise)
Under-12s Standing/Seating: £2.00

DISABLED INFORMATION

Wheelchairs: Accommodated
Helpers: Admitted
Prices: Normal prices apply
Disabled Toilets: Available
Contact (01903) 239575

Travelling Supporters' Information:
Routes: Take the A24/A27 to Worthing and at the Warren (or Grove Lodge) roundabout take the exit towards the Town Centre. Turn immediately right to keep Broadwater Green on your left and follow into South Farm Road. Go straight on at the next 5 mini-roundabouts then take the 3rd turning on the right into Pavilion Road. Turn right for Woodside Road.

YEOVIL TOWN FC

Founded: 1895
Former Names: Yeovil & Petters United FC
Nickname: 'Glovers'
Ground: Huish Park Stadium, Lufton Way, Yeovil, Somerset BA22 8YF
Ground Capacity: 9,565
Seating Capacity: 5,309
Record Attendance: 9,527 (25th April 2008)
Colours: Green and White shirts with White shcrts
Telephone Nº: (01935) 423662
Ticket Office Nº: (01935) 847888
Web site: www.ytfc.net
E-mail: info@ytfc.net

GENERAL INFORMATION

Car Parking: Spaces for 800 cars at the ground (£3.00)
Coach Parking: At the ground
Nearest Railway Station: Yeovil Pen Mill (2½ miles) and Yeovil Junction (3½ miles)
Nearest Bus Station: Yeovil (2 miles)
Club Shop: At the ground
Opening Times: Weekdays 10.00am – 4.00pm and Matchdays 10.00am – 3.00pm
Telephone Nº: (01935) 423662

GROUND INFORMATION

Away Supporters' Entrances & Sections:
Away Terrace (turnstiles 13-16) and Screwfix Community Stand (turnstile 12)

ADMISSION INFO (2023/2024 PRICES)

Adult Standing: £16.00
Adult Seating: £18.00 – £22.00
12s to 15s Standing/Seating: £5.00
Ages 16 to 21 Standing/Seating: £12.00
Senior Citizen/Armed Forces Standing: £14.00
Senior Citizen/Armed Forces Seating: £16.00
Under 12s Standing/Seating: £3.00
Note: Discounted prices are available for tickets which are purchased before the day of the match.

DISABLED INFORMATION

Wheelchairs: 15 spaces for home fans, 5 spaces for away fans
Helpers: Admitted free of charge
Prices: Concessionary prices apply for disabled fans
Disabled Toilets: Two are available
Contact: (01935) 423662 (Bookings are recommended). James Hillier – jhillier@tyfc.net

Travelling Supporters' Information:
Routes: From London: Take the M3 and A303 to Cartgate Roundabout. Enter Yeovil on the A3088. Exit left at the 1st roundabout then straight over the next two roundabouts into Western Avenue. Cross the next roundabout then turn left into Copse Road, where supporters' parking is sited; From the North: Exit the M5 at Junction 25 and take the A358 (Ilminster) and A303 (Eastbound) entering Yeovil on the A3088. Then as above.

National League 2022/2023 Season	Aldershot	Altrincham	Barnet	Boreham Wood	Bromley	Chesterfield	Dagenham & Redbridge	Dorking Wanderers	Eastleigh	FC Halifax Town	Gateshead	Maidenhead United	Maidstone United	Notts County	Oldham Athletic	Scunthorpe United	Solihull Moors	Southport	Torquay United	Wealdstone	Woking	Wrexham	Yeovil Town	York City
Aldershot Town		1-1	3-1	0-1	0-1	1-1	0-2	2-0	0-0	5-1	2-3	1-2	1-3	0-3	1-1	2-1	1-4	2-0	1-1	1-2	1-2	3-4	1-1	2-1
Altrincham	1-0		0-2	0-2	1-2	1-2	2-2	4-1	2-1	2-1	0-1	3-2	1-1	0-2	1-0	2-2	4-1	1-0	2-2	0-1	3-1	1-2	2-2	2-1
Barnet	4-1	2-4		2-1	1-1	3-0	0-2	0-1	3-1	2-0	1-1	2-1	4-3	1-1	1-3	1-1	1-0	0-3	1-0	2-0	2-0	0-0	2-1	0-5
Boreham Wood	1-2	1-1	1-1		0-2	1-0	0-1	1-0	0-0	1-1	0-2	1-0	3-1	2-2	2-1	2-0	1-1	1-0	0-1	1-0	0-1	1-1	1-0	1-1
Bromley	2-2	0-0	1-3	1-1		2-0	1-1	2-0	2-1	1-1	1-1	1-1	3-0	1-1	3-0	1-0	4-0	0-0	1-0	3-3	0-2	1-2	4-1	0-3
Chesterfield	1-0	1-0	3-1	2-0	3-2		2-3	3-1	3-2	2-0	2-1	1-2	4-0	1-2	0-1	4-1	2-0	3-2	5-1	1-1	1-3	2-0	1-1	1-3
Dagenham & Redbridge	2-1	4-1	5-4	1-1	4-1	0-1		0-2	0-1	0-0	2-2	1-0	1-0	0-5	1-1	2-1	2-1	1-1	0-1	4-1	1-2	0-4	0-2	2-1
Dorking Wanderers	0-3	3-2	2-1	1-4	2-3	2-2	5-1		1-1	0-0	2-1	3-1	3-2	3-1	1-5	2-1	0-3	1-0	3-2	3-1	1-2	0-5	1-1	1-0
Eastleigh	3-3	3-2	0-2	1-0	0-0	2-1	1-1	4-0		1-0	2-5	1-0	5-2	0-2	1-0	2-0	0-0	2-1	1-0	1-0	1-0	0-2	1-1	1-0
FC Halifax Town	2-0	2-2	1-3	1-0	1-1	1-0	2-0	3-1	1-1		2-0	0-1	3-0	1-4	2-1	0-1	1-1	0-0	0-1	5-0	0-4	3-1	1-1	1-0
Gateshead	0-2	1-3	2-2	1-1	0-3	1-2	3-0	0-0	1-1	0-0		4-0	4-1	1-1	2-1	2-0	1-1	3-1	1-1	0-1	1-3	0-3	4-0	2-2
Maidenhead United	1-1	2-0	1-1	0-1	1-0	0-0	2-1	1-1	2-1	1-1	0-1		2-1	3-4	1-1	3-2	0-2	1-2	1-3	0-0	1-0	2-2	2-0	0-1
Maidstone United	0-3	2-3	0-0	0-4	2-3	1-2	0-1	2-4	1-3	1-1	1-1	3-2		2-5	0-0	1-1	0-0	0-3	1-0	1-1	1-2	2-3	1-1	2-1
Notts County	2-0	3-1	4-1	1-1	1-1	2-2	1-2	3-1	3-1	1-0	2-0	3-0	3-0		4-1	4-0	1-0	4-0	4-0	3-0	3-0	1-0	0-0	1-1
Oldham Athletic	2-1	2-2	0-2	0-2	1-1	0-2	4-2	3-2	3-2	0-1	2-2	1-0	2-0	2-2		2-2	1-1	2-0	3-2	1-2	1-0	1-2	2-0	2-0
Scunthorpe United	3-3	2-0	1-3	0-2	1-1	1-2	3-2	3-2	0-1	0-2	3-1	3-0	0-2	1-4	0-2		3-4	1-3	0-1	4-1	0-2	1-3	2-1	1-1
Solihull Moors	1-2	5-1	1-1	2-0	2-2	0-0	0-3	3-0	3-0	0-1	0-2	1-1	2-0	1-2	2-1	3-1		1-1	3-2	2-1	0-1	1-2	2-2	1-1
Southend United	1-2	2-2	0-1	0-1	0-1	1-2	2-0	2-0	1-3	2-1	1-0	2-0	2-0	2-2	1-0	3-0	3-0		1-2	2-1	1-1	0-0	1-0	2-0
Torquay United	6-1	4-4	2-1	0-1	1-2	1-5	1-2	3-3	2-0	1-0	1-1	2-3	1-0	1-2	0-0	1-1	1-4	1-2		1-2	1-3	1-1	1-1	3-2
Wealdstone	0-1	4-0	0-2	1-2	3-2	0-4	1-0	2-2	3-1	1-0	1-2	3-2	2-1	1-6	2-2	3-1	3-0	0-1	1-1		1-1	0-0	0-0	3-1
Woking	4-1	1-1	1-1	2-2	2-1	0-1	2-0	3-3	1-0	0-1	2-1	2-0	3-1	2-3	3-0	2-0	2-0	1-1	1-1	1-1		2-3	1-0	0-2
Wrexham	2-0	4-0	7-5	3-1	2-1	2-1	4-1	3-1	2-1	3-1	3-1	1-0	5-0	3-2	5-1	2-0	5-0	1-0	6-0	3-1	2-2		3-0	3-0
Yeovil Town	0-2	1-1	1-2	1-1	0-1	2-2	1-0	0-1	1-0	1-0	3-1	0-0	2-2	1-4	0-3	0-0	1-0	0-2	2-0	0-0	0-1	1-1		0-1
York City	2-2	1-2	1-0	1-1	2-1	1-1	1-1	2-1	0-1	0-3	0-3	1-2	4-1	1-3	1-1	0-0	2-3	0-2	1-0	1-2	2-0	1-1	2-1	

National League

Season 2022/2023

Wrexham	**46**	**34**	**9**	**3**	**116**	**43**	**111**
Notts County	**46**	**32**	**11**	**3**	**117**	**42**	**107**
Chesterfield	46	25	9	12	81	52	84
Woking	46	24	10	12	71	48	82
Barnet	46	21	11	14	75	67	74
Boreham Wood	46	19	15	12	52	40	72
Bromley	46	18	17	11	68	53	71
Southend United	46	20	9	17	57	45	69
Eastleigh	46	19	10	17	56	57	67
Dagenham & Redbridge	46	18	9	19	61	72	63
FC Halifax Town	46	16	13	17	49	48	61
Oldham Athletic	46	16	13	17	63	64	61
Wealdstone	46	16	12	18	57	72	60
Gateshead	46	15	15	16	67	62	59
Solihull Moors	46	15	13	18	62	66	58
Dorking Wanderers	46	16	9	21	67	91	57
Altrincham	46	14	14	18	68	82	56
Aldershot Town	46	14	11	21	64	76	53
York City	46	13	12	21	55	63	51
Maidenhead United	46	13	11	22	47	66	50
Torquay United	***46***	***12***	***12***	***22***	***58***	***80***	***48***
Yeovil Town	***46***	***7***	***19***	***20***	***35***	***60***	***40***
Scunthorpe United	***46***	***8***	***10***	***28***	***49***	***87***	***34***
Maidstone United	***46***	***5***	***10***	***31***	***45***	***104***	***25***

National League Promotion Play-offs

Boreham Wood .... 2 Yeovil Town 0

Halifax Town .... 1 Barnet 2

Harrogate Town .... 1 Notts County 2

Boreham Wood .... 0 Barnet 0

Harrogate Town .... 3 Notts County 1

Barnet .... 1 Woking 1

Boreham Wood .... 2 Bromley 2

Notts County .... 3 Chesterfield 3

Boreham Wood .... 2 (aet) Bromley .... 2 (aet)

Notts County .... 2 Chesterfield .... 2 (aet)

Notts County won 4-3 on penalties.

Promoted: Wrexham and Notts County

Relegated: Torquay United, Yeovil Town, Scunthorpe United and Maidstone United

National League North 2022/2023 Season	AFC Fylde	AFC Telford United	Alfreton Town	Banbury United	Blyth Spartans	Boston United	Brackley Town	Bradford Park Avenue	Buxton	Chester	Chorley	Curzon Ashton	Darlington	Farsley Celtic	Gloucester City	Hereford United	Kettering Town	Kidderminster Harriers	King's Lynn Town	Leamington	Peterborough Sports	Scarborough Athletic	Southport	Spennymoor Town
AFC Fylde		3-1	2-0	5-0	0-3	4-1	3-0	3-1	1-0	1-1	1-2	3-1	3-2	3-1	2-0	1-3	2-1	0-2	3-3	5-1	1-0	0-2	1-0	2-2
AFC Telford United	0-3		1-2	2-1	0-1	1-2	0-1	4-0	1-1	0-0	1-0	2-3	1-4	1-1	0-4	0-1	1-1	1-2	0-4	1-1	0-1	1-1	1-1	1-1
Alfreton Town	0-1	1-0		2-0	1-0	3-1	1-0	0-0	3-0	2-2	0-2	1-2	2-2	1-0	1-2	1-1	2-0	1-1	0-2	2-0	2-2	2-0	4-0	3-2
Banbury United	3-1	1-2	1-1		0-0	0-0	0-1	1-0	1-3	2-2	3-0	0-0	0-0	2-2	1-1	3-1	0-3	0-1	0-1	2-2	0-0	2-1	3-1	0-1
Blyth Spartans	0-0	3-0	2-2	1-1		1-4	1-1	0-1	0-3	0-2	1-2	2-2	0-0	1-1	2-0	5-0	1-0	0-1	0-0	2-2	1-1	1-2	1-0	1-3
Boston United	0-1	4-1	1-0	0-1	3-0		1-0	1-0	3-0	2-3	1-4	0-1	3-1	4-0	2-2	2-4	1-1	2-1	0-2	3-0	0-0	2-2	3-5	1-2
Brackley Town	1-1	1-2	1-1	1-1	1-1	1-0		4-1	2-0	1-1	1-1	1-0	3-0	0-3	4-0	2-1	3-0	2-0	1-1	1-2	2-0	2-0	1-0	2-1
Bradford (Park Avenue)	0-2	1-0	3-0	1-0	0-1	2-1	1-2		1-4	1-2	0-0	2-1	1-3	1-1	2-1	1-0	1-1	0-1	0-1	3-1	1-2	0-0	2-0	0-1
Buxton	2-2	0-2	0-0	0-4	1-2	1-0	3-1	2-3		0-0	2-2	1-0	2-1	2-0	2-1	0-1	2-2	1-1	1-0	1-1	3-0	0-1	1-0	2-1
Chester	0-1	1-1	1-1	4-2	1-0	1-0	2-0	1-0	4-0		0-0	2-2	0-1	2-2	1-1	0-1	4-0	2-0	3-3	1-1	0-1	2-2	1-0	1-2
Chorley	0-1	1-0	0-0	1-0	1-1	2-3	0-0	0-0	2-2	2-2		3-0	1-1	4-3	3-0	2-0	2-0	1-0	0-1	1-0	1-0	2-3	1-2	2-0
Curzon Ashton	0-2	3-0	0-1	1-2	0-2	2-2	3-1	0-0	2-1	1-2	2-1		0-2	5-2	4-3	1-3	1-0	0-1	1-1	0-0	3-0	2-3	1-1	1-0
Darlington	1-2	3-1	3-1	1-2	1-0	3-2	2-2	2-2	1-1	1-2	0-3	0-2		1-0	3-1	3-0	2-2	0-0	1-3	1-1	2-0	2-3	0-0	3-2
Farsley Celtic	1-2	0-0	0-0	3-1	0-2	0-2	2-1	2-2	2-1	0-2	0-0	1-1	3-1		2-1	1-0	2-0	0-1	2-0	1-1	1-1	2-4	0-3	2-2
Gloucester City	1-2	3-0	1-1	1-1	2-2	2-0	0-1	5-1	0-1	1-1	4-3	0-3	2-6	5-1		2-0	2-0	1-1	2-1	1-1	3-1	2-3	3-2	2-0
Hereford	2-1	0-0	0-0	2-3	3-0	1-1	2-2	0-0	2-0	1-2	1-1	0-2	1-2	2-0	1-3		1-0	0-1	0-1	0-0	0-1	2-0	2-0	3-3
Kettering Town	0-0	2-0	1-3	0-0	4-2	3-2	1-0	1-1	0-0	0-1	3-3	1-0	0-0	0-0	0-1	2-0		0-3	1-0	3-0	0-0	1-1	0-0	2-1
Kidderminster Harriers	0-0	3-0	0-0	0-2	3-1	0-0	1-2	1-1	1-0	0-2	1-0	1-2	1-2	0-2	0-1	1-1	3-0		1-1	0-0	2-0	0-1	0-2	4-1
King's Lynn Town	0-1	3-0	3-2	3-1	2-0	2-1	2-1	2-1	1-1	0-1	2-0	2-0	3-0	1-2	1-1	2-1	4-1	3-0		1-1	2-1	3-2	3-2	3-0
Leamington	2-1	2-2	1-2	1-0	0-1	0-2	0-0	1-0	0-1	0-0	1-2	4-1	2-1	4-0	1-1	2-0	1-0	0-0	0-3		0-2	1-1	2-1	0-1
Peterborough Sports	0-2	3-2	1-2	3-2	4-0	1-1	2-0	1-0	1-1	3-2	0-0	0-0	0-1	1-0	1-2	0-2	1-2	1-2	1-2	3-0		0-1	2-1	1-1
Scarborough Athletic	1-2	1-0	2-0	3-3	3-2	1-1	0-0	2-2	0-1	1-3	3-2	0-1	2-5	1-2	0-3	1-0	5-0	4-2	3-3	4-1	2-1		0-1	2-2
Southport	1-2	0-0	0-0	1-2	2-1	1-1	2-2	4-1	1-4	1-2	2-1	2-1	1-0	4-0	0-1	0-1	0-0	1-3	1-1	1-0	0-3	1-1		1-3
Spennymoor Town	2-1	1-1	0-0	2-1	2-1	3-2	1-1	3-2	0-1	0-3	2-1	0-0	1-1	2-1	3-0	1-0	4-2	1-2	2-2	1-0	3-3	2-2	0-1	

National League North

Season 2022/2023

AFC Fylde	**46**	**29**	**8**	**9**	**80**	**44**	**95**
King's Lynn Town	46	27	12	7	84	43	93
Chester	46	22	18	6	72	41	84
Brackley Town	46	18	15	13	57	47	69
Alfreton Town	46	17	18	11	54	44	69
Kidderminster Harriers	**46**	**19**	**12**	**15**	**49**	**42**	**69**
Gloucester City	46	19	11	16	75	68	68
Scarborough Athletic	46	18	14	14	74	69	68
Spennymoor Town	46	18	14	14	68	67	68
Darlington	46	18	13	15	72	64	67
Buxton	46	18	13	15	55	54	67
Chorley	46	17	15	14	62	50	66
Curzon Ashton	46	18	11	17	58	55	65
Peterborough Sports	46	15	12	19	50	55	57
Boston United	46	15	11	20	68	66	56
Hereford	46	15	10	21	47	56	55
Banbury United	46	13	15	18	55	62	54
Southport	46	13	11	22	50	62	50
Blyth Spartans	46	12	14	20	49	62	50
Farsley Celtic	46	12	14	20	51	75	50
Kettering Town	***46***	***11***	***16***	***19***	***41***	***63***	***49***
Leamington	***46***	***10***	***18***	***18***	***41***	***60***	***48***
Bradford Park Avenue	***46***	***11***	***13***	***22***	***43***	***65***	***46***
AFC Telford United	***46***	***6***	***14***	***26***	***35***	***76***	***32***

National League North Promotion Play-offs

Alfreton Town .... 0 Kidderminster Harriers 1
Brackley Town .... 2 Gloucester City .... 2 (aet)
Gloucester City won 5-3 on penalties.

King's Lynn Town .... 1 Kidderminster Harriers 4
Chester .... 0 Brackley Town 1

Brackley Town .... 0 Kidderminster Harriers 2

Promoted: AFC Fylde and Kidderminster Harriers

Relegated: Kettering Town, Leamington, Bradford Park Avenue and AFC Telford United

National League South 2022/2023 Season	Bath City	Braintree Town	Chelmsford City	Cheshunt	Chippenham Town	Concord Rangers	Dartford	Dover Athletic	Dulwich Hamlet	Eastbourne Borough	Ebbsfleet United	Farnborough	Hampton & Richmond	Havant & Waterlooville	Hemel Hempstead Town	Hungerford Town	Oxford City	Slough Town	St. Albans City	Taunton Town	Tonbridge Angels	Welling United	Weymouth	Worthing
Bath City		3-1	0-1	1-0	1-3	4-0	0-2	0-1	2-1	2-0	1-3	0-1	1-1	2-0	1-0	2-3	2-1	5-1	1-3	0-2	0-1	1-1	2-1	2-2
Braintree Town	2-1		2-2	1-1	1-1	1-0	1-1	1-3	3-2	2-0	3-2	0-0	1-0	1-1	3-1	3-2	0-0	1-1	1-0	0-2	2-0	4-1	0-0	2-1
Chelmsford City	0-2	2-0		2-0	0-1	1-0	1-0	0-0	5-1	5-0	0-1	3-2	0-2	3-4	2-1	5-1	1-0	2-0	1-1	1-2	1-0	0-1	3-1	4-2
Cheshunt	2-1	0-5	1-2		3-2	4-2	1-3	2-0	0-3	1-0	1-0	0-1	3-2	2-3	0-0	0-1	1-2	1-1	1-2	0-0	3-4	1-1	1-0	0-2
Chippenham Town	0-0	1-2	0-0	4-4		2-2	2-1	3-1	2-1	1-1	0-0	2-1	2-1	0-3	0-1	1-0	1-0	0-1	1-1	3-1	2-2	3-2	3-2	1-1
Concord Rangers	0-2	1-3	1-2	1-1	3-1		3-2	1-0	1-1	2-4	1-2	0-1	2-0	3-4	2-1	1-0	1-2	0-2	1-2	1-0	1-0	1-1	0-5	1-1
Dartford	0-0	4-1	1-2	2-1	2-0	3-1		2-1	4-0	2-1	4-0	3-1	2-1	1-2	1-3	2-0	0-0	1-0	2-1	0-1	2-0	5-1	3-0	1-2
Dover Athletic	0-0	3-1	0-0	0-3	1-1	0-3	1-3		1-2	2-1	1-2	1-1	0-3	1-0	4-0	1-0	1-5	3-0	1-1	1-0	1-2	0-0	0-2	0-3
Dulwich Hamlet	1-2	2-1	2-1	1-0	0-1	0-0	1-2	1-1		1-3	1-3	1-4	3-2	2-1	1-3	2-1	2-2	1-2	1-0	2-0	1-2	1-2	2-0	0-1
Eastbourne Borough	3-4	1-2	2-2	3-0	2-1	2-1	2-1	3-1	2-1		2-3	2-0	0-1	1-3	3-0	3-1	1-1	2-0	1-0	0-3	1-2	0-1	5-1	0-2
Ebbsfleet United	3-1	4-0	2-0	3-0	3-0	4-1	1-4	3-0	4-2	0-2		4-2	6-2	2-0	0-0	5-0	3-0	2-0	3-1	5-0	1-2	1-1	4-1	7-2
Farnborough	0-1	0-1	0-1	3-0	0-1	2-1	3-1	3-0	1-1	0-0	2-2		2-2	2-2	1-2	2-1	2-1	4-1	1-2	1-0	1-2	0-0	3-1	0-1
Hampton & Richmond	1-1	0-3	2-1	2-1	1-0	3-0	0-0	0-2	2-0	3-2	1-2	0-1		2-3	1-1	2-0	1-1	0-1	0-6	3-1	0-1	1-1	2-1	0-0
Havant & Waterlooville	2-2	3-1	3-0	1-1	1-1	2-0	1-3	4-2	5-1	1-2	0-1	1-0	1-1		2-0	4-1	0-1	3-1	1-2	3-2	1-1	0-3	2-2	1-5
Hemel Hempstead Town	1-0	1-1	0-0	0-1	1-1	3-0	0-2	0-0	1-1	1-2	1-1	1-0	2-0	2-0		3-2	0-3	1-1	1-3	1-1	1-0	2-3	2-1	1-1
Hungerford Town	1-2	2-1	1-1	1-2	1-1	0-1	1-1	1-0	1-1	2-0	0-1	1-1	0-1	1-1	3-0		1-3	2-1	3-0	0-1	0-1	0-0	1-1	0-0
Oxford City	3-3	2-2	3-1	1-0	5-3	5-0	1-1	3-1	2-2	1-3	1-1	1-2	2-0	1-1	2-2	2-0		1-3	2-1	2-1	4-0	3-0	3-1	3-0
Slough Town	0-3	1-1	0-2	3-1	6-1	0-0	1-2	1-1	4-3	1-5	0-1	2-0	2-1	1-3	0-2	4-0	2-2		1-3	1-0	1-1	0-3	2-3	1-1
St Albans City	3-0	0-2	3-0	1-1	1-1	1-0	1-1	1-0	1-2	2-3	1-2	2-0	2-1	2-0	2-1	0-0	0-1	1-2		0-0	2-3	3-0	3-2	0-1
Taunton Town	1-1	0-0	0-0	1-0	3-1	1-0	2-1	0-1	1-1	1-2	0-1	0-2	1-3	2-0	1-2	0-3	1-1	2-1	0-1		4-1	0-0	1-3	3-2
Tonbridge Angels	1-2	0-0	1-0	1-0	2-0	2-2	0-1	4-0	3-1	3-0	1-1	2-1	1-4	1-1	1-1	4-3	2-2	3-3	1-2	2-3		0-1	0-5	2-1
Welling United	1-0	0-2	1-2	2-1	1-1	0-1	2-2	1-1	2-4	1-0	3-2	1-2	3-0	2-2	0-1	1-0	5-0	0-0	0-3	0-1	2-1		1-2	2-4
Weymouth	1-0	1-0	1-2	0-0	0-1	1-2	3-1	0-2	2-1	0-1	2-3	0-1	2-1	0-2	0-0	2-5	0-2	2-0	0-0	1-3	1-3	2-1		0-3
Worthing	2-3	2-1	1-3	3-2	0-0	7-0	3-0	1-1	6-0	1-1	0-6	1-2	4-3	3-2	3-1	2-1	1-0	2-2	4-5	1-1	3-2	3-2	1-3	

National League South

Season 2022/2023

Ebbsfleet United	**46**	**32**	**7**	**7**	**110**	**47**	**103**
Dartford	46	25	8	13	82	50	83
Oxford City	**46**	**21**	**15**	**10**	**83**	**56**	**78**
Worthing	46	22	12	12	92	72	78
Chelmsford City	46	23	9	14	67	49	78
St. Albans City	46	22	9	15	72	51	75
Braintree Town	46	20	14	12	66	55	74
Eastbourne Borough	46	22	5	19	74	66	71
Tonbridge Angels	46	20	10	16	68	69	70
Havant & Waterlooville	46	19	12	15	80	70	69
Bath City	46	19	10	17	64	57	67
Farnborough	46	19	9	18	59	52	66
Chippenham Town	46	15	17	14	57	66	62
Taunton Town	46	17	10	19	50	55	61
Hemel Hempstead Town	46	15	15	16	49	57	60
Welling United	46	15	14	17	57	63	58
Hampton & Richmond Borough	46	15	9	22	59	71	54
Slough Town	46	13	12	21	58	78	51
Weymouth	46	14	6	26	59	78	48
Dover Athletic	46	12	12	22	42	68	48
Dulwich Hamlet	***46***	***13***	***9***	***24***	***61***	***89***	***48***
Concord Rangers	***46***	***12***	***8***	***26***	***45***	***85***	***44***
Cheshunt	***46***	***11***	***10***	***25***	***48***	***74***	***43***
Hungerford Town	***46***	***10***	***10***	***26***	***48***	***72***	***40***

Welling United had 1 point deducted for fielding an ineligible player.

National League South Promotion Play-offs

Chelmsford City .... 0 St. Albans City .... 1 (aet)
Worthing .... 2 Braintree Town 1

Dartford .... 1 St. Albans City .... 1 (aet)
St. Albans City won 5-3 on penalties.
Oxford City .... 2 Worthing 0

Oxford City .... 4 St. Albans City 0

Promoted: Ebbsfleet United and Oxford City

Relegated: Dulwich Hamlet, Concord Rangers, Cheshunt and Hungerford Town

Northern Premier League Premier Division 2022/2023 Season	South Shields	Warrington Town	Bamber Bridge	Gainsborough Trinity	Matlock Town	Hyde United	Radcliffe	FC United of Manchester	Marine	Warrington Rylands 1906	Lancaster City	Stafford Rangers	Guiseley	Ashton United	Whitby Town	Marske United	Morpeth Town	Atherton Collieries	Nantwich Town	Stalybridge Celtic	Liversedge	Belper Town
South Shields		2-1	5-0	1-1	1-1	0-1	0-0	1-2	2-1	1-0	2-0	2-0	2-1	3-3	4-2	4-2	1-0	0-0	3-2	2-0	5-2	2-1
Warrington Town	3-2		1-0	0-2	3-1	3-1	1-0	0-1	0-0	3-3	2-0	2-0	0-0	3-0	2-2	0-1	2-0	1-1	2-1	1-1	3-1	3-1
Bamber Bridge	2-1	3-2		1-1	5-1	1-0	1-3	2-1	1-1	1-0	2-1	2-1	2-1	1-2	2-1	2-2	1-0	2-0	1-0	1-1	2-2	5-1
Gainsborough Trinity	1-1	1-1	1-2		3-0	1-1	2-2	1-2	1-0	2-0	0-2	0-0	1-1	2-0	0-1	6-2	1-1	2-2	0-1	4-0	4-0	2-2
Matlock Town	0-0	0-0	1-0	1-1		1-1	2-2	1-0	3-2	4-2	1-0	3-1	0-1	1-1	1-0	4-1	2-2	1-0	1-1	1-1	1-2	4-0
Hyde United	0-1	2-2	7-0	1-0	0-1		1-1	1-0	4-0	0-1	1-2	1-0	2-1	0-1	0-0	1-0	1-2	1-1	1-0	0-1	4-2	2-0
Radcliffe	1-2	0-3	2-0	1-1	1-0	1-0		1-0	1-1	0-3	2-2	0-0	4-2	1-1	1-1	2-4	3-1	0-2	1-2	2-1	2-0	4-2
FC United of Manchester	2-1	1-1	5-2	1-3	2-1	4-4	1-2		1-1	2-2	1-1	0-1	1-0	4-0	2-2	2-1	4-2	1-2	0-0	1-1	2-3	2-0
Marine	2-2	1-2	2-3	0-2	0-1	0-0	0-1	3-0		1-3	0-0	1-0	1-3	1-1	2-0	1-0	4-2	4-0	0-3	1-0	5-0	2-1
Warrington Rylands 1906	0-1	1-2	2-0	0-3	1-2	2-4	4-0	0-0	1-0		2-1	1-1	2-1	0-3	2-0	3-0	2-0	0-0	0-1	1-0	1-0	3-1
Lancaster City	0-2	0-1	1-1	1-2	2-1	2-1	0-0	2-0	1-3	2-1		1-2	2-1	1-0	2-0	2-0	2-1	0-0	1-1	1-1	0-0	1-1
Stafford Rangers	3-0	1-1	4-2	3-4	0-2	1-1	1-0	1-0	2-1	2-2	2-1		1-1	1-1	1-0	2-0	0-0	1-2	3-0	0-3	2-0	1-2
Guiseley	1-0	1-3	0-1	0-1	2-1	2-3	1-3	2-1	0-3	1-1	0-0	4-0		1-2	2-1	1-3	1-0	3-0	2-1	1-1	1-0	0-1
Ashton United	1-1	2-1	3-0	2-3	0-1	0-6	1-2	0-5	1-1	3-1	2-4	1-1	2-0		0-1	1-2	1-0	3-0	0-1	2-1	1-2	3-1
Whitby Town	0-1	2-1	3-0	0-6	4-1	1-1	0-0	0-2	0-3	1-0	1-2	0-1	0-2	2-1		2-1	0-1	1-0	1-1	0-1	2-3	2-2
Marske United	0-4	1-2	1-2	0-3	2-1	0-2	0-2	0-2	0-1	2-0	2-3	3-2	2-4	2-1	0-0		2-1	2-3	2-2	4-2	2-2	3-1
Morpeth Town	0-1	0-4	1-1	2-0	2-0	3-0	0-1	0-1	0-2	3-3	6-3	2-1	1-3	3-1	0-1	1-1		3-0	2-1	3-2	0-2	0-2
Atherton Collieries	0-2	1-1	0-3	1-1	0-1	0-1	1-1	1-0	0-1	2-0	1-1	1-2	2-1	2-0	1-3	2-0	1-1		2-0	1-1	0-4	1-1
Nantwich Town	0-1	1-1	0-1	1-1	0-1	0-1	2-1	0-2	1-2	2-2	2-1	1-1	0-1	1-2	0-2	1-2	3-0	2-1		0-4	0-1	1-0
Stalybridge Celtic	3-3	0-1	1-0	2-0	2-3	2-2	1-2	1-2	0-0	1-2	1-0	0-2	0-0	1-4	0-1	2-3	0-3	3-3	1-2		4-2	2-1
Liversedge	0-1	0-4	1-2	1-0	0-2	1-3	1-1	0-4	1-0	2-5	1-1	3-3	2-1	0-1	0-3	0-1	1-4	0-1	3-3	0-1		1-3
Belper Town	0-1	1-1	0-2	1-4	1-1	1-1	1-1	1-4	1-2	0-5	1-2	2-1	1-3	0-4	2-2	0-1	1-2	2-0	1-3	2-0	1-2	

Northern Premier League – Premier Division

Season 2022/2023

South Shields	**42**	**25**	**10**	**7**	**71**	**39**	**85**
Warrington Town	**42**	**21**	**14**	**7**	**70**	**39**	**77**
Bamber Bridge	42	22	7	13	62	63	73
Gainsborough Trinity	42	18	15	9	74	41	69
Matlock Town	42	19	11	12	56	49	68
Hyde United	42	18	12	12	64	42	66
Radcliffe	42	17	15	10	55	49	66
FC United of Manchester	42	19	9	14	68	48	63
Marine	42	17	10	15	56	45	61
Warrington Rylands 1906	42	17	9	16	64	55	60
Lancaster City	42	15	13	14	51	51	58
Stafford Rangers	42	15	12	15	52	53	57
Guiseley	42	16	7	19	54	54	55
Ashton United	42	16	8	18	58	64	53
Whitby Town	42	14	10	18	45	54	52
Marske United	42	15	5	22	57	79	50
Morpeth Town	42	14	7	21	55	63	49
Atherton Collieries	42	11	14	17	38	57	47
Nantwich Town	***42***	***12***	***10***	***20***	***44***	***55***	***46***
Stalybridge Celtic	***42***	***10***	***12***	***20***	***50***	***64***	***42***
Liversedge	***42***	***11***	***7***	***24***	***48***	***86***	***40***
Belper Town	***42***	***7***	***9***	***26***	***44***	***86***	***30***

FC United of Manchester had three points deducted after mistakenly fielding 6 loan players in a game.
Ashton United had three points deducted after fielding an ineligible player.

Southern Football League Premier Division Central 2022/2023 Season	AFC Rushden & Diamonds	Alvechurch	Barwell	Basford United	Bedford Town	Bromsgrove Sporting	Coalville Town	Hednesford Town	Hitchin Town	Ilkeston Town	Kings Langley	Leiston	Mickleover	Needham Market	Nuneaton Borough	Redditch United	Royston Town	Rushall Olympic	St. Ives Town	Stourbridge	Stratford Town	Tamworth
AFC Rushden & Diamonds		0-2	0-1	2-0	4-0	1-1	0-7	0-1	1-2	1-1	4-2	0-0	1-4	0-0	2-1	0-2	1-1	1-3	2-1	1-3	0-2	1-3
Alvechurch	2-0		2-1	2-1	2-0	0-0	0-3	1-0	1-3	2-1	2-2	3-3	2-1	1-1	1-3	3-3	2-1	1-2	4-1	3-0	4-2	1-3
Barwell	1-2	1-1		2-2	1-2	1-1	3-1	5-1	1-2	2-1	0-0	2-3	2-5	2-0	3-1	1-0	2-1	1-2	3-1	1-1	2-1	0-2
Basford United	2-1	3-0	0-4		3-1	1-1	0-2	1-0	0-2	2-1	0-1	2-0	1-2	2-1	0-4	0-1	3-1	1-1	1-0	2-1	0-2	1-3
Bedford Town	6-1	0-3	3-2	0-2		3-4	2-1	1-3	3-0	2-2	2-0	3-4	0-3	0-1	0-2	0-1	0-2	0-2	1-3	2-4	0-3	1-8
Bromsgrove Sporting	1-1	3-1	2-0	1-1	2-2		0-4	3-1	2-1	2-3	2-0	1-7	1-3	2-0	3-0	0-1	2-1	0-1	1-2	3-4	0-1	0-1
Coalville Town	3-0	4-1	3-2	0-1	2-0	1-1		3-2	5-1	1-4	2-1	0-0	4-1	1-0	0-2	2-2	2-2	3-1	3-0	3-1	1-1	1-0
Hednesford Town	5-0	1-2	2-2	0-0	1-2	2-3	1-3		1-0	2-2	1-0	1-3	0-3	4-0	1-2	0-1	3-3	0-0	2-2	0-0	2-0	0-1
Hitchin Town	2-1	2-1	1-1	0-0	0-0	2-0	2-2	1-1		3-1	2-4	0-3	4-1	1-0	1-1	2-1	1-0	0-0	1-1	1-1	1-0	0-1
Ilkeston Town	3-1	3-0	2-0	1-1	3-2	3-1	1-2	4-1	3-1		3-0	2-2	2-3	3-3	2-3	1-1	3-3	1-1	2-3	0-2	2-1	0-2
Kings Langley	1-2	1-1	0-2	1-1	3-1	2-5	1-3	2-1	0-1	1-2		1-1	2-2	0-2	1-2	2-0	1-0	0-1	0-1	2-3	1-1	1-1
Leiston	5-1	1-1	2-0	6-2	3-0	3-2	1-0	1-0	0-0	2-1	1-2		3-1	2-1	3-2	2-1	3-0	2-1	1-0	1-1	1-1	2-1
Mickleover	2-0	1-0	2-3	2-1	2-0	4-1	2-4	1-1	1-2	1-1	2-0	2-2		2-0	3-1	2-1	1-0	2-0	3-2	1-1	4-3	2-3
Needham Market	2-0	0-3	1-2	3-2	0-0	0-1	0-0	1-0	3-0	1-3	1-2	0-1	2-0		1-1	1-0	5-0	0-2	4-2	3-1	0-1	3-2
Nuneaton Borough	2-1	3-1	3-1	1-0	2-1	4-0	0-1	2-1	1-1	2-0	1-1	2-1	4-2	1-1		1-0	3-1	0-0	3-0	0-0	1-0	1-1
Redditch United	1-0	1-0	1-3	2-1	3-0	2-0	0-1	1-1	2-1	1-4	2-3	3-1	2-1	3-1	1-2		4-2	2-3	2-0	0-3	2-2	0-3
Royston Town	2-1	1-0	2-4	3-1	3-2	4-0	1-1	2-0	4-2	1-2	1-0	1-1	1-1	1-0	1-0	0-0		2-1	1-3	3-3	4-2	0-2
Rushall Olympic	3-1	1-4	1-1	0-1	1-3	3-1	0-3	3-0	3-1	2-0	2-1	0-2	1-3	1-0	3-0	7-2	2-3		1-0	2-0	4-3	2-2
St Ives Town	3-1	3-1	1-1	2-2	2-0	1-2	1-3	2-0	3-2	2-2	2-0	1-2	2-0	1-1	1-2	1-2	0-2	0-2		1-5	5-0	2-0
Stourbridge	0-2	0-2	0-1	1-2	2-1	1-1	2-3	3-1	3-0	1-2	2-1	1-1	1-2	0-0	0-0	0-3	5-1	2-0	2-2		4-0	1-1
Stratford Town	2-0	2-0	1-1	2-2	1-1	4-2	1-0	1-0	1-2	1-1	1-2	1-1	2-1	4-2	1-1	2-0	1-1	0-5	3-3	1-1		0-4
Tamworth	2-2	3-0	4-1	2-1	2-2	1-0	1-4	9-1	2-1	1-1	3-0	3-1	3-1	0-1	3-0	0-0	3-0	3-1	2-1	0-3	2-0	

Southern Football League
Premier Division Central

Season 2022/2023

Tamworth	**42**	**27**	**8**	**7**	**93**	**40**	**89**
Coalville Town	42	27	8	7	92	42	89
Leiston	42	24	13	5	84	47	85
Nuneaton Borough	42	23	10	9	67	45	79
Rushall Olympic	**42**	**22**	**7**	**13**	**71**	**52**	**73**
Mickleover	42	22	6	14	82	66	72
Ilkeston Town	42	16	13	13	79	66	61
Barwell	42	17	10	15	69	63	61
Redditch United	42	18	7	17	57	59	61
Stourbridge	42	15	14	13	69	56	59
Alvechurch	42	17	8	17	63	65	59
Hitchin Town	42	16	11	15	52	60	59
Royston Town	42	15	10	17	63	73	55
Stratford Town	42	13	13	16	58	70	52
Basford United	42	14	10	18	49	62	52
St. Ives Town	42	14	8	20	64	72	50
Needham Market	42	13	9	20	46	54	48
Bromsgrove Sporting	42	13	9	20	58	78	48
Kings Langley	***42***	***10***	***9***	***23***	***45***	***69***	***39***
Hednesford Town	***42***	***7***	***10***	***25***	***45***	***76***	***31***
AFC Rushden & Diamonds	***42***	***8***	***7***	***27***	***40***	***87***	***31***
Bedford Town	***42***	***8***	***6***	***28***	***49***	***93***	***30***

Hednesford Town resigned from the league at the end of the season.

Southern Football League Premier Division South 2022/2023 Season	Beaconsfield Town	Bracknell Town	Chesham United	Dorchester Town	Gosport Borough	Hanwell Town	Harrow Borough	Hartley Wintney	Hayes & Yeading United	Hendon	Merthyr Town	Metropolitan Police	North Leigh	Plymouth Parkway	Poole Town	Salisbury	Swindon Supermarine	Tiverton Town	Truro City	Weston-super-Mare	Winchester City	Yate Town
Beaconsfield Town		2-3	5-2	0-1	3-2	2-2	1-3	1-0	5-2	1-1	3-5	2-2	3-3	3-1	0-2	2-1	2-3	1-2	3-2	1-0	0-1	3-2
Bracknell Town	3-1		0-3	2-0	3-1	1-1	4-1	5-0	2-2	3-2	1-0	3-2	6-0	0-0	0-2	6-1	4-2	2-1	0-3	2-2	3-1	0-3
Chesham United	4-2	2-1		2-0	2-1	2-2	2-2	1-0	0-3	2-0	1-2	3-2	1-0	4-0	2-2	3-1	1-1	3-0	3-1	1-1	1-1	5-1
Dorchester Town	0-2	1-2	1-3		2-2	3-0	3-2	4-2	1-3	3-2	0-2	1-0	2-1	3-1	1-6	1-0	3-4	1-2	1-0	0-3	2-1	2-0
Gosport Borough	3-2	0-4	2-3	2-2		0-2	1-3	1-0	3-2	1-0	3-2	0-2	2-0	5-1	1-2	0-0	3-1	2-1	0-1	0-4	2-2	0-1
Hanwell Town	1-1	2-3	2-0	2-1	4-1		1-1	3-2	3-2	1-1	0-2	0-1	5-1	1-0	0-2	0-3	1-3	1-0	1-3	0-1	1-2	3-1
Harrow Borough	1-0	0-4	2-1	1-2	0-2	0-1		1-0	1-2	1-3	1-2	0-2	1-0	0-1	2-1	0-1	1-3	2-2	1-4	1-5	1-1	3-1
Hartley Wintney	0-3	1-2	1-5	2-4	3-1	2-1	1-0		0-0	2-3	1-2	1-1	1-0	4-4	1-1	1-3	0-3	1-2	0-1	0-0	1-1	3-0
Hayes & Yeading United	2-2	2-1	0-3	4-0	3-2	1-0	2-2	1-2		1-0	3-2	3-2	3-1	2-1	1-1	1-0	0-0	7-0	3-4	0-1	4-0	3-0
Hendon	1-1	3-4	0-0	0-0	2-0	1-0	3-0	1-0	1-2		1-1	2-3	0-2	3-1	0-4	1-4	2-2	2-2	2-2	2-3	0-2	0-1
Merthyr Town	3-2	1-3	0-1	1-3	2-3	3-1	2-2	4-1	1-3	1-2		1-2	0-3	0-1	1-2	5-0	2-1	2-0	2-1	2-3	5-2	1-2
Metropolitan Police	2-3	0-1	1-0	1-3	2-1	2-0	1-3	3-1	2-1	2-1	0-2		1-1	1-0	1-3	0-3	1-0	4-1	1-2	0-0	2-1	0-1
North Leigh	0-2	0-5	2-3	2-0	0-1	2-0	2-0	3-0	1-1	0-2	0-2	0-2		1-2	0-4	1-1	1-2	4-2	1-2	2-0	2-4	3-3
Plymouth Parkway	1-1	1-3	2-2	3-0	2-0	1-1	4-0	0-0	3-1	6-0	0-1	0-1	1-1		4-0	3-1	2-1	4-2	3-3	1-4	1-0	2-1
Poole Town	2-2	2-2	3-3	3-0	1-1	3-2	1-0	1-0	2-1	4-3	2-0	1-1	2-1	0-0		1-2	2-2	2-4	3-0	1-3	1-0	5-0
Salisbury	1-0	2-1	1-2	2-2	1-3	2-0	0-0	1-3	0-2	3-3	1-2	1-4	4-2	0-1	1-3		2-1	0-1	0-3	1-1	1-2	0-0
Swindon Supermarine	1-1	1-2	5-3	3-2	3-1	1-1	2-1	1-0	3-5	4-1	2-1	4-2	2-1	3-0	2-1	1-0		3-3	3-2	0-0	1-2	2-0
Tiverton Town	1-2	1-1	2-1	3-0	1-0	2-3	0-0	1-0	0-0	1-0	2-2	3-2	2-1	1-1	2-1	2-4	1-3		1-1	0-2	2-4	4-2
Truro City	1-1	1-0	3-1	4-0	1-0	1-0	2-1	1-1	1-0	4-1	0-0	2-0	6-0	1-3	1-1	4-0	4-0	3-2		0-0	3-0	4-0
Weston-super-Mare	2-2	1-3	1-3	3-1	3-0	3-0	7-0	4-0	1-0	4-1	1-0	1-1	3-0	1-0	2-0	3-1	3-1	2-1	0-1		3-1	3-2
Winchester City	4-0	2-3	1-1	1-1	0-1	0-3	0-0	2-1	3-0	1-1	2-2	1-1	2-2	2-1	0-3	0-1	1-6	1-2	1-3	0-1		1-0
Yate Town	0-2	0-2	0-3	0-0	5-4	2-3	3-3	0-1	1-2	2-1	2-2	2-1	1-3	4-0	2-3	0-4	1-2	0-0	1-2	0-4	3-3	

Southern Football League Premier Division South

Season 2022/2023

Weston-super-Mare	**42**	**28**	**9**	**5**	**89**	**32**	**93**
Bracknell Town	42	28	6	8	100	53	90
Truro City	**42**	**27**	**8**	**7**	**88**	**41**	**89**
Poole Town	42	23	11	8	86	51	80
Chesham United	42	23	10	9	88	57	79
Swindon Supermarine	42	23	8	11	88	66	77
Hayes & Yeading United	42	21	8	13	80	58	71
Metropolitan Police	***42***	***18***	***7***	***17***	***61***	***59***	***61***
Merthyr Town	42	18	6	18	73	64	60
Plymouth Parkway	42	16	10	16	63	62	58
Beaconsfield Town	42	15	12	15	75	73	57
Tiverton Town	42	15	10	17	62	77	55
Dorchester Town	42	16	6	20	57	79	54
Hanwell Town	42	14	8	20	55	65	50
Salisbury	42	14	7	21	55	71	49
Winchester City	42	12	12	18	56	72	48
Gosport Borough	42	14	5	23	58	78	47
Hendon	42	9	11	22	55	81	38
Harrow Borough	42	9	10	23	44	80	37
North Leigh	***42***	***9***	***7***	***26***	***50***	***86***	***34***
Yate Town	***42***	***9***	***7***	***26***	***50***	***92***	***34***
Hartley Wintney	***42***	***8***	***8***	***26***	***40***	***76***	***32***

Metropolitan Police took voluntary relegation to Step 4 and joined the Isthmian League South Central Division.

Isthmian League Premier Division 2022/2023 Season	Aveley	Billericay Town	Bishop's Stortford	Bognor Regis Town	Bowers & Pitsea	Brightlingsea Regent	Canvey Island	Carshalton Athletic	Corinthian-Casuals	Cray Wanderers	Enfield Town	Folkestone Invicta	Haringey Borough	Hastings United	Herne Bay	Hornchurch	Horsham	Kingstonian	Lewes	Margate	Potters Bar Town	Wingate & Finchley
Aveley		1-0	0-1	1-6	2-0	1-1	0-1	0-0	2-1	0-1	1-1	2-1	3-0	2-1	1-1	1-0	0-1	0-0	2-0	3-1	3-1	1-0
Billericay Town	2-0		2-2	3-2	3-2	4-1	1-0	1-1	1-2	2-1	0-4	2-3	3-1	1-0	2-0	0-3	5-3	5-1	2-1	3-0	2-0	0-1
Bishop's Stortford	2-0	2-0		2-0	2-0	3-0	2-2	2-0	3-0	1-1	4-1	3-0	2-1	2-3	3-0	4-1	1-1	1-0	0-3	2-2	1-1	0-0
Bognor Regis Town	1-1	0-1	2-1		2-1	4-2	0-1	3-3	3-2	2-2	0-2	2-0	0-1	0-0	2-1	1-0	0-2	2-4	1-4	1-0	1-2	3-0
Bowers & Pitsea	2-1	0-0	0-1	0-4		1-1	1-1	0-1	1-0	1-2	1-4	3-1	2-1	0-2	2-1	0-2	0-0	2-2	2-3	0-2	2-0	2-2
Brightlingsea Regent	0-6	2-0	2-0	0-4	0-2		1-5	1-1	4-2	0-1	0-4	3-2	1-1	2-3	1-2	1-1	0-2	0-1	2-2	2-1	0-0	1-2
Canvey Island	2-2	1-2	2-0	3-2	0-2	3-0		1-1	2-1	1-1	3-0	3-0	1-1	3-1	3-2	2-1	1-3	3-0	1-3	5-2	5-0	0-3
Carshalton Athletic	1-0	2-0	0-2	2-1	1-0	2-1	0-2		1-0	1-1	1-3	1-0	0-1	2-1	1-3	2-2	1-1	1-0	2-1	1-0	5-2	3-1
Corinthian-Casuals	1-3	1-2	0-1	1-2	4-1	2-1	0-0	1-4		1-3	0-3	0-4	0-2	0-2	3-2	2-2	1-2	0-2	1-1	0-1	1-2	1-0
Cray Wanderers	2-1	4-3	2-3	2-2	3-3	4-0	1-0	2-1	1-0		1-1	0-0	5-1	0-1	3-0	0-2	5-3	2-0	2-2	1-0	5-0	0-1
Enfield Town	1-2	2-0	0-1	1-1	2-0	2-1	0-0	4-1	2-0	1-1		1-1	2-2	1-0	4-2	1-1	2-1	0-1	2-4	0-0	4-1	1-1
Folkestone Invicta	2-5	1-1	3-0	4-1	4-1	3-1	1-3	0-0	3-2	2-4	3-0		2-1	0-0	2-1	1-2	3-0	1-3	1-2	4-0	2-3	2-1
Haringey Borough	1-2	0-3	0-3	2-5	4-2	6-1	1-2	1-0	2-2	2-2	1-2	3-0		2-0	2-4	1-1	2-0	5-2	1-2	1-0	1-2	0-0
Hastings United	1-2	2-2	0-1	3-2	2-0	4-1	1-1	1-0	3-0	1-0	1-1	2-1	4-1		3-3	0-3	0-0	1-0	2-1	0-0	1-2	1-1
Herne Bay	1-2	2-2	0-5	2-1	3-1	1-1	1-4	2-3	3-1	3-5	1-3	1-2	0-1	0-3		0-6	3-0	1-1	4-1	1-1	1-3	1-1
Hornchurch	1-2	1-0	2-1	1-0	2-0	4-1	1-3	1-1	5-0	2-1	3-2	2-1	3-3	3-0	5-1		3-1	3-0	2-2	2-3	5-0	2-0
Horsham	2-2	3-1	0-2	4-0	4-1	6-1	2-0	1-3	5-0	2-2	3-1	1-3	3-3	0-0	4-1	3-2		1-0	2-0	4-0	3-2	2-0
Kingstonian	0-1	2-1	0-5	2-2	1-0	3-0	1-4	2-1	1-2	0-1	0-0	2-0	0-3	0-3	1-1	1-2	1-4		1-3	0-2	1-3	2-2
Lewes	1-1	1-1	2-1	3-1	2-2	2-0	0-2	2-0	2-0	0-0	1-0	3-2	4-0	0-0	3-3	2-2	1-1	3-0		2-0	2-1	5-0
Margate	0-1	0-0	0-1	2-0	1-1	3-3	2-0	0-1	2-0	0-3	2-5	0-1	3-3	1-2	4-0	1-3	1-1	1-1	2-2		2-3	3-1
Potters Bar Town	0-2	3-0	0-1	0-2	1-0	3-1	1-2	3-1	0-1	1-1	2-1	0-5	2-2	1-4	1-0	2-5	1-1	3-2	4-3	0-1		0-2
Wingate & Finchley	1-2	1-3	0-1	4-2	4-3	5-0	0-2	3-0	1-1	1-0	0-2	0-2	0-0	0-4	4-1	2-4	2-2	2-2	1-1	1-2	2-0	

Isthmian League Premier Division

Season 2022/2023

Bishop's Stortford	**42**	**27**	**7**	**8**	**75**	**33**	**88**
Hornchurch	42	25	9	8	98	49	84
Canvey Island	42	24	9	9	80	44	81
Aveley	**42**	**23**	**9**	**10**	**64**	**42**	**78**
Cray Wanderers	42	20	14	8	78	48	74
Lewes	42	20	14	8	82	54	74
Horsham	42	20	12	10	84	57	72
Hastings United	42	20	11	11	63	42	71
Enfield Town	42	19	12	11	73	49	69
Billericay Town	42	19	8	15	66	59	65
Carshalton Athletic	42	18	10	14	53	53	64
Folkestone Invicta	42	18	5	19	73	65	59
Potters Bar Town	42	16	5	21	56	86	53
Bognor Regis Town	42	15	7	20	70	72	52
Haringey Borough	42	13	12	17	67	75	51
Wingate & Finchley	42	12	12	18	53	64	48
Margate	42	11	11	20	48	65	44
Kingstonian	42	10	9	23	43	77	39
Bowers & Pitsea	***42***	***8***	***9***	***25***	***44***	***78***	***33***
Herne Bay	***42***	***8***	***9***	***25***	***60***	***101***	***33***
Corinthian-Casuals	***42***	***7***	***5***	***30***	***37***	***87***	***26***
Brightlingsea Regent	***42***	***5***	***9***	***28***	***41***	***108***	***24***

Northern Premier League Division One West 2022/2023 Season	Macclesfield	Leek Town	Workington	Clitheroe	Runcorn Linnets	Witton Albion	Mossley	Kidsgrove Athletic	Prescot Cables	Trafford	Skelmersdale United	City of Liverpool	Bootle	1874 Northwich	Newcastle Town	Hanley Town	Widnes	Glossop North End	Colne	Ramsbottom United
Macclesfield		4-0	4-1	3-0	3-2	1-1	4-3	5-0	2-2	3-1	1-0	5-0	1-2	0-1	3-0	4-0	5-0	2-0	4-2	4-0
Leek Town	1-3		0-1	3-2	0-2	0-1	1-1	1-1	4-1	1-3	3-1	4-1	3-2	2-1	0-1	4-1	3-0	3-1	1-0	1-1
Workington	0-1	1-1		0-1	2-1	5-0	0-1	3-0	3-3	2-1	2-1	0-0	0-1	2-1	3-0	3-0	2-1	3-0	4-0	1-1
Clitheroe	1-1	1-0	1-1		0-1	4-1	2-1	1-3	2-2	1-2	0-1	3-2	4-0	1-3	7-1	4-3	4-2	3-2	4-1	2-0
Runcorn Linnets	2-1	0-1	1-3	1-2		1-0	1-2	2-0	2-0	2-1	3-0	0-2	1-1	2-2	3-1	0-0	3-1	0-0	2-0	5-0
Witton Albion	1-0	1-2	3-2	1-1	4-2		0-2	3-2	1-0	0-1	5-3	0-0	2-2	1-0	3-1	5-1	1-2	0-1	1-0	5-1
Mossley	1-3	0-2	1-3	1-1	1-0	1-1		1-2	2-1	2-2	1-2	2-1	1-0	3-0	1-1	2-1	4-1	3-0	1-1	1-0
Kidsgrove Athletic	0-3	0-1	1-3	2-1	0-1	1-1	2-2		2-0	0-1	1-2	2-0	2-1	3-3	0-0	1-2	1-1	1-0	2-1	2-1
Prescot Cables	1-2	1-4	1-1	0-2	1-0	2-1	2-1	0-0		1-2	2-1	1-1	2-2	2-1	0-0	4-0	0-1	2-0	0-0	3-1
Trafford	0-1	0-2	1-2	2-1	0-0	2-1	2-0	1-1	1-2		2-3	3-2	2-3	1-0	2-2	0-2	2-0	2-2	1-1	1-0
Skelmersdale United	1-4	2-4	1-2	0-1	1-4	0-1	1-0	1-2	3-2	2-3		2-4	2-4	0-2	1-3	1-2	2-0	0-2	2-1	1-0
City of Liverpool	0-1	0-5	3-0	2-0	1-1	1-1	0-0	2-1	0-1	3-2	1-2		1-1	1-2	1-2	1-0	4-0	0-3	1-0	2-1
Bootle	1-2	0-4	0-1	0-4	2-3	2-1	1-1	1-1	3-1	2-0	2-1	2-1		2-0	1-2	1-4	2-2	1-2	1-2	1-2
1874 Northwich	0-0	0-0	4-3	1-2	0-1	1-4	0-1	2-2	0-0	2-0	2-1	2-0	1-1		2-0	0-1	2-0	0-2	4-1	1-1
Newcastle Town	0-2	1-2	0-1	1-0	0-2	1-1	1-5	1-1	3-2	1-0	0-1	1-6	1-0	2-2		1-1	2-1	1-1	0-1	0-2
Hanley Town	1-1	0-0	1-2	1-1	2-2	0-0	1-1	2-2	0-1	1-2	2-4	2-3	2-0	4-0	1-2		0-2	1-0	2-2	0-0
Widnes	0-4	0-2	1-0	0-0	1-1	2-3	2-1	1-2	0-3	2-1	1-3	3-0	1-1	1-0	1-3	1-0		3-2	1-[illegible]	3-1
Glossop North End	1-2	1-1	0-3	1-2	1-1	2-2	2-3	2-1	1-1	0-0	1-2	1-0	0-3	0-1	4-1	2-4	1-1		0-1	2-1
Colne	1-1	0-1	2-3	2-1	1-0	1-1	2-3	0-2	0-2	2-2	1-2	2-1	1-1	1-0	1-2	1-2	0-1	3-0		2-1
Ramsbottom United	0-5	2-3	0-3	2-3	1-3	0-3	3-1	2-3	2-1	3-2	3-5	1-2	0-1	2-1	2-1	1-3	0-0	1-4	0-0	

Northern Premier League – Division One West

Season 2022/2023

Macclesfield	**38**	**28**	**6**	**4**	**95**	**27**	**90**
Leek Town	38	23	7	8	70	38	76
Workington	**38**	**23**	**6**	**9**	**71**	**39**	**75**
Clitheroe	38	19	7	12	70	50	64
Runcorn Linnets	38	18	9	11	58	38	63
Witton Albion	38	16	11	11	61	50	59
Mossley	38	16	10	12	58	49	58
Kidsgrove Athletic	38	13	12	13	49	55	51
Prescot Cables	38	13	11	14	50	51	50
Trafford	38	14	8	16	51	55	50
Skelmersdale United	***38***	***16***	***0***	***22***	***58***	***74***	***48***
City of Liverpool	38	13	7	18	50	59	46
Bootle	38	12	10	16	51	61	46
1874 Northwich	38	12	9	17	44	50	45
Newcastle Town	38	12	9	17	40	67	45
Hanley Town	38	11	11	16	50	61	44
Widnes	38	12	8	18	40	66	44
Glossop North End	***38***	***10***	***9***	***19***	***44***	***59***	***39***
Colne	***38***	***9***	***10***	***19***	***38***	***57***	***37***
Ramsbottom United	***38***	***7***	***6***	***25***	***39***	***81***	***27***

Skelmersdale United were relegated as they were unable to meet the FA ground grading regulations after their artificial pitch failed a "bounce test".

Northern Premier League Division One East 2022/2023 Season	Worksop Town	Stockton Town	Hebburn Town	Long Eaton United	Stocksbridge Park Steels	Dunston UTS	North Shields	Brighouse Town	Sheffield	Pontefract Collieries	Cleethorpes Town	Grimsby Borough	Consett	Bridlington Town	Ossett United	Grantham Town	Carlton Town	Lincoln United	Shildon	Tadcaster Albion
Worksop Town		1-0	4-1	7-1	4-1	3-1	4-0	4-0	1-0	3-2	0-0	5-0	3-1	2-2	1-1	2-0	4-0	6-0	6-0	4-1
Stockton Town	2-1		2-1	1-2	1-0	1-2	4-2	1-2	6-0	2-3	1-0	1-1	1-2	4-0	1-1	1-1	4-3	5-0	2-1	5-0
Hebburn Town	1-6	2-0		1-4	1-3	1-1	2-1	1-0	2-1	2-1	3-1	0-4	5-1	2-0	1-1	2-2	0-2	0-2	1-0	5-3
Long Eaton United	0-1	1-1	3-2		2-1	2-3	3-1	3-0	0-1	2-1	3-0	1-4	1-1	2-2	0-2	1-1	1-1	2-1	4-1	1-0
Stocksbridge Park Steels	0-2	1-2	4-1	0-1		2-2	1-1	1-1	1-0	2-0	3-0	0-0	0-1	3-0	1-3	1-0	2-0	2-3	2-0	1-0
Dunston UTS	1-1	1-1	0-1	0-2	2-3		1-1	4-0	2-0	3-3	3-2	2-1	4-2	1-1	3-3	1-1	1-3	3-1	2-1	4-1
North Shields	2-3	1-1	1-2	1-0	0-3	1-1		0-0	1-0	3-0	0-0	3-0	1-0	1-2	1-1	2-0	2-1	1-1	1-2	2-1
Brighouse Town	0-6	0-2	1-3	1-4	2-3	1-2	2-2		1-1	6-0	1-2	2-0	2-0	2-3	2-1	1-3	4-1	2-2	3-0	3-0
Sheffield	1-3	2-1	2-1	3-2	1-1	0-2	2-0	1-0		3-3	0-0	0-1	1-1	1-1	2-3	1-3	0-0	2-1	2-0	1-1
Pontefract Collieries	0-2	2-1	1-1	1-2	2-3	2-1	0-2	2-1	2-2		2-2	4-0	1-1	1-1	3-1	0-0	2-2	3-1	3-0	6-2
Cleethorpes Town	0-2	0-2	1-1	2-1	0-2	0-1	1-1	0-2	3-0	1-4		0-0	2-1	1-0	2-0	3-1	2-3	5-0	1-2	2-1
Grimsby Borough	2-2	1-1	0-1	1-3	1-1	1-0	0-5	3-5	1-4	2-0	0-0		2-2	5-2	0-1	3-1	1-2	3-3	2-3	1-0
Consett	1-2	3-4	0-2	0-3	1-2	2-1	0-0	1-4	3-0	3-1	3-2	1-3		2-3	1-1	2-2	5-0	4-2	1-0	2-1
Bridlington Town	2-2	1-0	1-2	1-1	1-0	1-2	2-1	1-0	1-1	0-5	0-3	1-0	0-0		2-2	0-0	0-0	1-3	1-1	2-0
Ossett United	1-2	0-3	0-1	0-3	1-0	0-2	0-3	0-4	0-3	2-2	1-2	3-1	1-1	2-1		0-0	1-2	1-1	1-1	4-1
Grantham Town	0-1	1-1	0-1	0-1	0-1	0-0	1-0	3-0	2-3	0-0	0-1	0-3	3-0	1-0	0-4		0-1	3-3	3-1	2-0
Carlton Town	0-3	0-2	0-2	2-0	1-3	2-0	1-2	2-4	2-4	1-0	1-1	0-2	2-1	2-4	0-2	0-2		1-4	0-2	1-1
Lincoln United	0-1	1-2	3-1	3-1	1-0	2-1	0-1	1-1	3-3	2-2	1-1	0-2	0-1	1-3	1-1	0-1	1-0		1-2	4-0
Shildon	1-4	0-3	1-2	2-2	3-2	0-2	2-3	1-2	1-2	0-0	3-1	1-1	1-3	6-0	1-0	1-0	0-4	1-1		3-1
Tadcaster Albion	0-4	0-2	1-1	2-2	0-2	1-1	1-0	0-3	2-1	0-4	2-4	0-2	0-0	3-2	0-0	0-0	0-2	1-0	1-1	

Northern Premier League – Division One East

Season 2022/2023

Worksop Town	**38**	**31**	**6**	**1**	**112**	**25**	**99**
Stockton Town	38	20	8	10	74	40	68
Hebburn Town	38	20	6	12	59	58	66
Long Eaton United	**38**	**19**	**8**	**11**	**67**	**52**	**65**
Stocksbridge Park Steels	38	19	6	13	58	41	63
Dunston UTS	38	16	12	10	63	50	60
North Shields	***38***	***14***	***11***	***13***	***50***	***45***	***53***
Brighouse Town	38	15	6	17	65	64	51
Sheffield	38	13	11	14	51	58	50
Pontefract Collieries	38	12	13	13	68	62	49
Cleethorpes Town	38	13	10	15	48	51	49
Grimsby Borough	38	13	10	15	54	60	49
Consett	38	12	10	16	54	63	46
Bridlington Town	38	11	13	14	45	65	46
Ossett United	38	10	14	14	46	55	44
Grantham Town	38	10	13	15	37	42	43
Carlton Town	38	12	6	20	45	69	42
Lincoln United	***38***	***10***	***11***	***17***	***54***	***70***	***41***
Shildon	***38***	***11***	***7***	***20***	***46***	***70***	***40***
Tadcaster Albion	***38***	***4***	***9***	***25***	***28***	***84***	***21***

North Shields were relegated to the Northern League after failing to prove they could provide stipulated ground improvements.

Northern Premier League Division One Midlands 2022/2023 Season	Bedworth United	Boldmere St. Michaels	Cambridge City	Chasetown	Coleshill Town	Corby Town	Daventry Town	Dereham Town	Gresley Rovers	Halesowen Town	Harborough Town	Hinckley LRFC	Loughborough Dynamo	Shepshed Dynamo	Spalding United	Sporting Khalsa	Stamford	St. Neots Town	Sutton Coldfield Town	Yaxley
Bedworth United		1-2	2-2	0-0	1-0	3-3	0-0	1-1	3-0	1-1	0-0	1-0	1-2	1-1	0-0	0-2	0-2	2-1	0-2	2-1
Boldmere St. Michaels	2-1		3-1	1-5	2-2	0-4	2-1	3-1	2-0	1-0	0-1	2-0	1-1	1-3	1-1	1-1	0-1	5-1	3-0	5-1
Cambridge City	0-0	1-1		0-4	2-3	2-0	1-1	1-2	3-0	1-2	0-3	1-1	2-1	1-4	0-0	1-1	1-2	1-1	0-1	2-1
Chasetown	2-1	0-1	0-1		0-2	1-1	1-0	2-0	3-0	0-0	0-0	1-0	3-0	1-0	1-0	2-0	1-2	4-0	3-1	1-0
Coleshill Town	1-0	2-0	1-2	1-1		0-0	3-2	3-0	2-0	3-2	2-4	2-1	3-1	0-2	1-1	1-0	3-1	4-0	3-0	2-0
Corby Town	1-1	3-2	1-1	0-4	1-0		2-1	3-0	2-2	4-2	0-4	1-0	0-2	0-0	1-0	2-2	1-1	4-0	3-1	4-1
Daventry Town	0-1	0-2	0-4	1-2	0-4	0-7		2-0	3-2	1-4	0-2	0-0	0-4	3-2	0-9	0-7	1-2	1-1	0-1	3-0
Dereham Town	0-2	0-3	1-0	2-3	1-4	0-1	6-0		2-0	0-3	3-2	1-1	1-1	0-3	0-2	1-3	1-3	0-1	3-2	6-2
Gresley Rovers	1-0	1-0	0-0	1-0	1-0	0-3	2-0	1-0		2-3	2-2	2-2	0-2	2-0	0-2	0-2	0-0	1-2	4-2	4-0
Halesowen Town	2-0	2-3	2-1	1-0	2-0	3-2	4-0	4-0	3-0		1-0	3-0	3-2	0-1	3-0	2-2	0-0	3-0	0-3	3-0
Harborough Town	2-2	4-2	1-0	1-0	2-2	1-0	2-1	6-1	1-0	1-3		1-0	3-0	2-1	0-2	2-3	0-2	1-1	2-1	9-1
Hinckley LRFC	1-0	2-1	2-0	0-1	4-1	0-1	1-0	2-1	4-0	2-2	0-0		1-1	0-1	1-1	1-2	0-1	1-1	3-0	2-1
Loughborough Dynamo	4-1	0-1	1-1	1-0	1-1	2-3	2-2	1-2	0-0	0-2	2-3	1-1		2-0	0-4	2-1	3-1	3-1	1-0	4-0
Shepshed Dynamo	1-1	2-0	0-1	1-2	0-2	0-3	3-0	2-2	0-1	3-4	1-2	0-1	2-0		0-2	3-0	0-2	3-1	3-0	1-1
Spalding United	2-2	2-2	0-2	3-2	0-1	2-2	3-0	2-0	4-0	3-0	3-1	0-1	0-0	1-0		2-0	3-2	1-0	1-0	4-2
Sporting Khalsa	0-0	2-2	1-2	1-1	1-0	4-1	7-1	5-0	1-0	0-5	5-1	3-1	1-0	1-3	2-1		0-2	2-0	2-1	8-0
Stamford	2-0	2-1	3-1	3-2	2-1	2-0	4-0	1-1	1-1	2-1	3-1	1-0	2-0	3-0	1-2	3-1		4-0	0-3	3-0
St. Neots Town	0-4	0-2	3-2	1-1	2-1	2-0	1-2	1-3	1-1	1-3	1-0	3-0	1-3	3-3	0-3	2-4	1-3		1-3	4-1
Sutton Coldfield Town	4-0	1-2	2-0	0-0	0-3	1-5	2-2	3-0	1-0	1-1	2-3	2-1	2-2	1-2	0-1	2-3	1-1	6-0		2-1
Yaxley	0-2	1-3	0-2	0-1	0-4	1-2	0-2	0-1	2-3	0-1	3-1	0-0	0-3	0-4	0-1	0-4	0-6	2-2	1-2	

Northern Premier League – Division One Midland

Season 2022/2023

Stamford	**38**	**27**	**6**	**5**	**76**	**31**	**87**
Halesowen Town	**38**	**24**	**6**	**8**	**80**	**40**	**78**
Spalding United	38	22	9	7	68	28	75
Sporting Khalsa	38	21	7	10	84	48	70
Coleshill Town	38	21	6	11	68	39	69
Chasetown	38	20	8	10	58	27	68
Corby Town	38	19	10	9	71	48	67
Harborough Town	38	20	7	11	71	50	67
Boldmere St Michaels	38	19	7	12	65	51	64
Loughborough Dynamo	38	14	10	14	55	50	52
Shepshed Dynamo	38	15	6	17	55	47	51
Sutton Coldfield Town	38	14	5	19	56	60	47
Hinckley LRFC	38	11	11	16	37	40	44
Cambridge City	38	11	11	16	43	51	44
Bedworth United	38	9	15	14	37	45	42
Gresley Rovers	38	11	8	19	34	58	41
Dereham Town	***38***	***10***	***5***	***23***	***43***	***79***	***35***
St. Neots Town	***38***	***8***	***8***	***22***	***41***	***87***	***32***
Daventry Town	***38***	***6***	***6***	***26***	***30***	***100***	***24***
Yaxley	***38***	***1***	***3***	***34***	***23***	***116***	***6***

Southern Football League Division One Central 2022/2023 Season	Aylesbury United	Barton Rovers	Berkhamstead	Biggleswade	Biggleswade Town	Cirencester Town	Didcot Town	AFC Dunstable	FC Romania	Hadley	Hertford Town	Highworth Town	Kempston Rovers	Kidlington	Thame United	Waltham Abbey	Walthamstow	Ware	Welwyn Garden City
Aylesbury United		2-1	0-4	0-2	1-3	0-1	0-1	1-1	2-1	1-0	0-0	5-1	1-3	2-0	0-2	0-2	0-2	2-1	1-2
Barton Rovers	0-2		1-4	2-2	0-1	0-2	1-0	0-2	1-2	0-1	3-1	2-2	2-2	1-0	1-2	0-2	0-3	0-4	0-1
Berkhamsted	4-0	5-0		1-0	1-0	3-2	2-0	4-0	6-1	2-1	2-0	5-0	3-1	0-0	1-0	2-1	2-1	0-2	2-2
Biggleswade	0-2	4-3	2-2		0-1	3-1	2-0	3-1	8-0	2-3	4-1	0-2	2-2	4-1	2-0	2-1	0-0	3-3	1-0
Biggleswade Town	4-1	5-1	1-2	0-2		0-0	1-2	3-2	5-3	3-3	2-2	4-1	2-2	2-2	3-2	2-0	1-1	4-2	2-3
Cirencester Town	3-0	0-2	3-4	4-1	0-1		2-0	1-0	3-0	2-2	2-1	1-1	5-0	2-0	1-2	3-3	6-1	3-0	1-2
Didcot Town	1-1	0-0	0-4	1-0	1-0	1-0		3-2	4-1	0-1	2-1	2-2	1-0	0-0	2-2	3-2	1-0	0-3	0-1
AFC Dunstable	0-0	4-0	2-4	1-2	1-1	2-0	0-1		5-1	1-1	4-4	3-0	0-0	1-3	1-2	1-0	3-0	3-0	3-1
FC Romania	4-1	1-1	2-1	0-1	0-0	1-2	2-5	0-1		4-1	2-1	4-1	0-2	0-1	0-0	0-1	0-0	1-3	0-4
Hadley	4-3	3-0	1-2	1-2	4-2	1-0	1-3	0-0	1-1		3-1	5-3	3-2	1-2	2-1	2-0	0-1	0-2	1-1
Hertford Town	4-4	2-1	3-1	2-2	1-3	1-0	3-5	0-0	5-0	1-1		2-2	1-2	2-1	4-2	2-3	4-1	1-2	0-2
Highworth Town	1-2	3-3	1-4	2-2	0-3	0-4	0-6	1-1	5-0	1-0	2-3		3-3	0-1	1-0	1-0	2-3	2-2	2-4
Kempston Rovers	1-2	1-2	0-1	1-2	2-0	0-3	1-2	0-3	2-1	1-4	3-2	1-1		0-1	3-0	0-2	2-3	1-2	5-0
Kidlington	2-2	0-0	0-4	0-4	0-1	2-0	1-2	1-1	3-0	3-2	0-4	5-1	1-1		1-0	1-2	0-1	4-1	5-2
Thame United	1-1	2-0	2-2	2-2	2-3	1-1	3-1	1-2	7-2	4-1	2-1	4-0	3-1	0-2		1-3	0-1	1-2	2-2
Waltham Abbey	0-1	5-1	0-2	0-1	3-3	1-1	1-3	2-1	2-2	2-0	2-1	3-1	1-2	1-1	1-3		2-3	0-1	1-1
Walthamstow	2-1	1-1	1-2	0-1	3-2	0-0	1-0	2-0	6-0	0-4	1-4	2-0	3-2	0-1	0-2	3-2		3-0	0-0
Ware	3-0	5-1	2-0	2-2	3-1	3-4	0-1	2-1	3-0	2-2	4-2	1-4	4-1	3-0	1-1	0-3	4-6		1-2
Welwyn Garden City	3-0	2-1	0-3	2-3	1-1	0-4	1-1	3-0	3-0	0-4	0-3	3-2	3-1	1-2	3-1	0-1	0-3	1-3	

Southern Football League
Division One Central

Season 2022/2023

Berkhamsted	**36**	**28**	**4**	**4**	**91**	**32**	**88**
Biggleswade	36	20	9	7	73	44	69
Didcot Town	**36**	**20**	**6**	**10**	**55**	**42**	**66**
Walthamstow	36	19	6	11	58	49	63
Ware	36	19	5	12	76	60	62
Cirencester Town	36	17	7	12	67	39	58
Biggleswade Town	36	16	10	10	70	54	58
Welwyn Garden City	36	16	7	13	56	60	55
Hadley	36	15	8	13	64	55	53
Kidlington	36	15	8	13	47	48	53
Waltham Abbey	36	14	6	16	55	51	48
Thame United	36	13	8	15	60	54	47
AFC Dunstable	36	12	10	14	53	47	46
Hertford Town	36	11	8	17	70	70	41
Aylesbury United	36	11	7	18	41	64	40
Kempston Rovers	36	9	7	20	51	69	34
Highworth Town	**36**	**6**	**10**	**20**	**51**	**93**	**28**
Barton Rovers	36	5	8	23	32	78	23
FC Romania	**36**	**6**	**6**	**24**	**36**	**97**	**21**

FC Romania had three points deducted for fielding an ineligible player.

Harlow Town resigned from the League on 7th December 2022 and their record was expunged.

Southern Football League Division One South 2022/2023 Season	AFC Totton	Bashley	Bideford	Bishop's Cleeve	Bristol Manor Farm	Cinderford Town	Evesham United	Exmouth Town	Frome Town	Hamworthy United	Larkhall Athletic	Lymington Town	Melksham Town	Paulton Rovers	Sholing	Slimbridge	Tavistock	Westbury United	Willand Rovers	Wimborne Tnwn
AFC Totton		1-0	8-1	2-1	4-1	3-0	2-1	1-0	1-1	0-0	1-1	3-1	3-0	7-0	0-1	3-0	6-1	5-3	1-0	1-1
Bashley	0-0		0-1	0-4	2-1	3-0	0-0	1-1	1-0	0-1	3-0	1-0	0-2	1-0	1-3	0-1	0-1	0-0	2-1	5-2
Bideford	1-1	0-1		1-2	1-0	0-1	0-1	1-1	2-0	1-2	1-0	1-2	1-1	0-2	2-1	2-2	1-1	3-4	1-3	0-1
Bishop's Cleeve	1-2	1-0	1-2		2-4	2-2	1-0	2-2	0-2	1-5	4-2	2-3	3-1	2-1	0-2	3-2	4-2	2-1	1-0	3-6
Bristol Manor Farm	2-4	0-3	0-0	1-3		3-2	1-3	2-0	1-1	2-1	1-1	1-2	1-5	4-3	1-1	0-3	1-2	1-0	2-1	0-0
Cinderford Town	1-6	1-2	1-1	2-1	1-3		3-1	1-1	1-3	5-0	1-1	0-2	0-4	0-4	2-2	2-1	0-4	3-2	0-2	1-2
Evesham United	3-2	1-1	2-1	3-0	3-2	0-0		2-0	1-0	1-2	5-0	2-1	2-1	2-1	0-2	1-0	0-1	0-2	2-0	1-2
Exmouth Town	1-3	3-2	1-1	1-2	1-1	2-1	4-1		5-0	0-1	0-3	0-1	2-0	2-0	2-3	2-2	1-0	0-0	3-3	1-0
Frome Town	0-1	0-1	0-0	2-0	0-0	5-1	1-0	1-0		2-0	2-2	1-1	2-1	2-0	2-3	4-1	0-4	3-0	3-3	3-0
Hamworthy United	2-1	1-0	5-1	2-1	5-2	1-1	2-1	3-1	3-2		5-0	3-2	2-2	1-1	1-1	1-1	6-2	3-2	0-0	2-1
Larkhall Athletic	0-3	1-1	1-1	3-2	2-1	2-2	2-1	0-1	0-4	0-1		0-0	2-2	2-1	2-0	3-1	0-1	2-1	2-1	1-3
Lymington Town	1-2	3-3	0-2	2-2	2-4	1-2	2-0	0-2	0-0	1-0	2-1		3-2	0-1	1-1	2-0	3-7	3-0	3-1	0-2
Melksham Town	0-1	0-3	1-0	0-1	3-3	1-1	2-2	1-3	3-2	3-5	1-1	3-2		2-3	1-3	3-2	1-2	3-2	3-0	3-1
Paulton Rovers	0-1	2-1	3-2	2-4	3-1	5-2	3-2	1-0	3-2	0-1	2-4	4-1	1-3		0-2	3-2	1-4	1-1	0-0	1-1
Sholing	1-0	1-1	1-1	4-1	3-2	2-0	0-2	4-0	3-2	2-0	1-1	1-0	5-1	2-0		1-0	4-1	1-1	2-0	0-0
Slimbridge	0-1	1-1	2-3	1-3	1-1	2-3	2-2	0-4	0-1	4-2	0-1	1-0	1-2	1-1	1-3		2-4	0-1	0-4	1-0
Tavistock	0-0	0-2	2-0	4-1	1-3	2-0	1-2	3-1	4-3	0-2	0-1	3-1	0-1	1-0	3-2	1-1		1-2	0-3	1-2
Westbury United	1-2	2-1	2-3	1-0	0-1	4-1	0-2	1-1	1-0	2-1	0-0	1-1	1-1	0-1	3-2	3-0	1-1		1-0	2-1
Willand Rovers	1-2	1-1	0-1	2-2	4-0	2-2	0-1	1-0	2-2	3-3	0-0	3-0	1-0	2-1	0-1	0-2	3-1	0-0		1-0
Wimborne Town	0-4	0-5	1-1	2-1	3-2	3-1	0-0	2-1	1-4	2-0	2-0	5-1	1-1	3-2	0-4	3-3	2-0	3-3	2-1	

Southern Football League
Division One South

Season 2022/2023

AFC Totton	**38**	**27**	**7**	**4**	**88**	**28**	**88**
Sholing	**38**	**24**	**9**	**5**	**75**	**35**	**81**
Hamworthy United	38	22	8	8	75	51	74
Evesham United	38	18	6	14	53	44	60
Wimborne Town	38	17	9	12	60	61	60
Tavistock	38	18	4	16	66	63	58
Bashley	38	15	10	13	49	37	55
Frome Town	38	15	9	14	62	50	54
Bishop's Cleeve	38	16	4	18	66	74	52
Westbury United	38	13	11	14	51	53	50
Larkhall Athletic	38	12	13	13	44	58	49
Melksham Town	38	13	9	16	64	68	48
Paulton Rovers	38	14	5	19	57	68	47
Exmouth Town	38	12	10	16	50	51	46
Willand Rovers	38	11	11	16	49	47	44
Lymington Town	***38***	***12***	***7***	***19***	***50***	***67***	***43***
Bideford	38	10	12	16	41	57	42
Bristol Manor Farm	38	11	9	18	56	76	42
Cinderford Town	***38***	***8***	***10***	***20***	***47***	***85***	***34***
Slimbridge	***38***	***6***	***9***	***23***	***44***	***74***	***27***

Isthmian League North Division 2022/2023 Season	AFC Sudbury	Basildon United	Brentwood Town	Bury Town	Coggeshall Town	East Thurrock United	Felixstowe & Walton United	Gorleston	Grays Athletic	Great Wakering Rovers	Hashtag United	Heybridge Swifts	Hullbridge Sports	Lowestoft Town	Maldon & Tiptree	New Salamis	Stowmarket Town	Tilbury	Witham Town	Wroxham
AFC Sudbury		5-0	5-0	2-1	3-0	1-0	1-0	5-2	3-1	5-0	4-2	2-2	3-0	0-1	2-1	3-1	2-0	3-0	1-0	2-1
Basildon United	2-2		1-2	3-1	2-0	1-1	1-3	0-0	2-2	2-1	0-0	1-1	1-0	2-3	0-1	1-1	0-2	3-1	2-2	0-0
Brentwood Town	1-2	2-0		0-0	1-1	1-1	1-1	3-0	2-0	0-1	1-3	0-0	5-1	2-2	3-1	1-1	1-2	4-2	5-3	3-0
Bury Town	2-2	1-0	0-2		0-0	0-1	3-1	0-1	1-4	1-0	1-0	1-0	2-2	1-1	2-0	2-2	0-1	1-0	3-0	0-0
Coggeshall Town	0-1	2-1	0-1	1-2		2-4	1-3	4-0	0-0	1-0	1-2	0-0	1-3	1-3	0-0	2-0	0-5	1-1	0-1	0-2
East Thurrock United	2-4	0-1	1-0	1-0	1-2		2-2	2-0	1-2	2-0	0-4	0-1	1-1	1-0	0-4	2-2	1-2	1-2	1-0	0-2
Felixstowe & Walton U.	1-2	2-0	2-0	1-2	1-1	1-1		3-2	1-0	2-1	4-0	0-1	2-0	0-1	3-1	5-0	3-1	2-1	4-1	2-1
Gorleston	1-2	3-1	0-1	0-2	2-0	1-0	0-0		1-2	2-2	0-3	3-1	3-0	1-6	1-0	2-3	0-2	2-5	4-1	1-2
Grays Athletic	0-2	3-3	3-0	1-0	1-0	1-0	3-2	3-0		2-1	2-3	1-1	2-0	2-1	2-0	0-0	0-0	2-0	7-1	2-0
Great Wakering Rovers	2-1	1-1	1-2	1-2	2-1	2-4	0-4	2-4	1-2		0-3	0-1	3-0	0-3	0-0	1-2	1-4	0-1	0-4	3-3
Hashtag United	3-2	3-0	5-2	3-1	2-1	2-1	1-0	2-0	3-0	6-0		2-0	4-0	3-1	2-1	3-1	1-1	3-1	4-1	2-1
Heybridge Swifts	3-2	5-1	3-1	3-0	2-0	2-0	2-1	1-0	0-1	2-0	1-2		4-1	4-4	0-1	3-0	1-3	5-1	2-1	0-1
Hullbridge Sports	0-2	1-2	0-3	1-2	1-0	1-2	1-2	2-3	2-0	1-0	0-3	1-3		0-0	1-2	1-2	1-0	0-3	1-3	2-3
Lowestoft Town	0-2	3-2	3-3	2-2	4-0	2-0	2-1	5-2	3-1	5-4	0-2	1-1	4-2		2-1	2-0	2-1	2-0	4-0	2-2
Maldon & Tiptree	0-3	3-1	0-2	0-0	1-1	3-2	1-2	0-0	0-2	0-3	0-2	1-2	1-0	5-3		2-5	2-3	0-2	0-1	1-1
New Salamis	1-1	2-2	1-0	1-1	3-0	1-2	4-3	1-3	2-3	4-1	1-2	2-2	3-2	2-1	2-1		3-1	1-1	1-0	3-3
Stowmarket Town	1-0	0-1	1-0	2-0	1-2	2-2	2-3	2-2	2-0	2-2	3-1	1-2	4-1	0-3	1-0	2-2		2-1	2-0	1-0
Tilbury	1-2	2-2	1-1	1-0	0-0	1-2	1-3	0-1	0-2	3-4	1-8	0-1	0-3	0-2	0-1	1-2	0-3		0-2	1-1
Witham Town	0-2	1-2	1-1	1-0	2-2	0-1	0-2	3-0	2-1	2-3	0-4	0-2	1-1	0-3	2-4	1-1	2-1	0-1		4-1
Wroxham	1-5	1-0	1-0	0-0	2-0	2-3	2-2	0-2	0-2	3-3	2-3	1-1	2-1	0-3	0-1	2-0	2-0	5-0	2-0	

Isthmian League North Division

Season 2022/2023

Hashtag United	**38**	**32**	**2**	**4**	**101**	**35**	**98**
AFC Sudbury	**38**	**29**	**4**	**5**	**91**	**33**	**91**
Lowestoft Town	38	23	8	7	89	50	77
Heybridge Swifts	38	21	9	8	65	37	72
Grays Athletic	38	22	6	10	62	40	72
Felixstowe & Walton United	38	21	6	11	74	44	69
Stowmarket Town	38	20	6	12	63	44	66
Brentwood Town	38	15	10	13	57	50	55
New Salamis	38	14	13	11	63	65	55
Wroxham	38	13	11	14	52	55	50
Bury Town	38	13	11	14	37	41	50
East Thurrock United	38	14	7	17	46	55	49
Gorleston	38	13	5	20	49	71	44
Basildon United	38	9	13	16	44	63	40
Maldon & Tiptree	38	11	6	21	40	58	39
Witham Town	38	10	5	23	43	75	35
Coggeshall Town	***38***	***6***	***10***	***22***	***28***	***60***	***28***
Great Wakering Rovers	***38***	***7***	***6***	***25***	***46***	***87***	***27***
Tilbury	***38***	***7***	***6***	***25***	***36***	***77***	***27***
Hullbridge Sports	***38***	***6***	***4***	***28***	***35***	***81***	***22***

AFC Sudbury were promoted to the Southern League Premier Central division.

Isthmian League South Central Division 2022/2023 Season	Ashford Town	Basingstoke Town	Bedfont Sports	Binfield	Chertsey Town	Chipstead	Guernsey	Hanworth Villa	Leatherhead	Marlow	Merstham	Northwood	South Park	Southall	Sutton Common Rovers	Thatcham Town	Tooting & Mitcham United	Uxbridge	Walton & Hersham	Westfield
Ashford Town		0-3	1-0	0-1	2-2	1-4	4-2	2-2	0-3	0-3	3-2	2-1	3-1	1-3	2-1	3-3	2-1	4-3	0-5	0-5
Basingstoke Town	5-0		0-0	0-2	3-1	3-0	8-0	0-1	2-0	2-0	3-1	0-1	3-1	1-0	2-1	2-0	4-2	3-2	0-1	4-1
Bedfont Sports	2-2	1-3		1-2	0-0	0-0	6-0	0-0	0-1	2-2	4-2	0-1	0-2	1-4	3-3	0-0	0-0	2-1	3-2	0-0
Binfield	3-0	0-1	3-1		1-1	1-0	1-2	0-1	2-1	0-1	4-0	0-0	4-2	1-1	3-2	2-2	4-1	2-1	0-2	1-2
Chertsey Town	6-1	0-3	1-1	1-2		3-0	4-0	1-1	3-1	0-2	0-1	0-1	4-0	2-2	1-0	0-3	2-1	1-0	2-5	3-0
Chipstead	1-2	2-4	2-1	1-1	2-0		1-2	0-2	1-3	0-0	1-1	1-0	0-1	0-0	3-4	3-1	2-0	2-1	0-2	1-0
Guernsey	0-1	2-3	1-1	3-1	3-3	2-2		3-1	1-1	2-3	1-2	1-2	1-0	4-1	1-0	0-1	0-2	0-2	0-0	0-1
Hanworth Villa	1-1	0-4	2-1	2-2	0-4	2-5	3-0		0-0	1-2	2-1	2-1	2-1	2-0	3-1	3-2	3-1	2-2	0-2	2-2
Leatherhead	2-1	0-0	2-1	2-2	1-3	2-3	1-2	1-0		0-2	2-1	2-0	0-1	0-0	4-3	2-0	1-1	0-0	0-2	0-4
Marlow	4-2	5-2	3-2	2-2	0-1	3-0	1-1	2-0	1-3		1-1	3-0	1-3	1-1	1-2	1-1	2-0	1-1	4-3	3-0
Merstham	2-0	1-5	2-2	0-2	1-1	1-0	2-2	0-1	1-2	0-0		1-0	1-2	1-2	3-0	1-1	0-0	1-1	3-3	2-2
Northwood	3-1	0-1	1-2	0-0	3-1	0-0	2-1	1-4	3-1	3-1	3-2		0-2	2-0	2-1	2-0	3-2	1-0	1-2	2-1
South Park	1-0	0-1	4-3	3-1	0-3	0-2	2-2	1-2	1-0	2-0	1-1	3-1		1-0	1-0	2-4	1-1	2-1	2-0	1-1
Southall	2-0	0-1	1-0	2-1	4-1	1-4	3-0	2-0	1-0	1-0	3-3	1-2	2-2		2-2	2-2	1-1	1-2	3-2	1-1
Sutton Common Rovers	1-0	0-5	0-3	0-3	0-5	0-1	0-1	2-1	1-1	1-3	2-0	1-5	4-0	1-1		2-2	3-0	0-2	1-0	0-2
Thatcham Town	1-0	0-2	5-1	0-4	2-1	2-3	0-0	1-2	1-2	1-1	1-1	2-1	3-0	1-0	1-2		2-0	2-0	2-2	2-2
Tooting & Mitcham United	2-3	2-3	2-1	2-0	1-2	1-1	1-0	0-3	0-1	0-1	0-0	0-2	1-1	0-1	0-2	1-2		2-2	1-4	0-2
Uxbridge	6-1	1-2	2-3	4-3	2-0	1-0	1-1	1-1	0-2	0-1	3-0	1-0	2-2	2-1	0-0	2-0	0-4		1-3	1-1
Walton & Hersham	3-1	5-1	4-1	5-1	3-2	3-1	6-0	1-2	0-2	3-0	6-0	2-1	4-0	3-0	2-0	3-2	2-1	3-1		2-1
Westfield	1-0	4-0	1-1	2-1	0-2	3-3	0-1	0-2	1-1	2-3	0-1	1-3	3-1	0-0	2-2	2-1	2-2	1-1	1-2	

Isthmian League South Central Division

Season 2022/2023

Basingstoke Town	**38**	**29**	**2**	**7**	**89**	**37**	**89**
Walton & Hersham	**38**	**28**	**3**	**7**	**102**	**41**	**87**
Marlow	38	19	10	9	64	45	67
Hanworth Villa	38	19	9	10	58	50	66
Northwood	38	20	3	15	54	45	63
Binfield	38	16	9	13	63	51	57
Leatherhead	38	16	9	13	47	45	57
Chertsey Town	38	16	8	14	67	52	56
South Park	38	16	7	15	50	61	55
Southall	38	13	13	12	50	48	52
Chipstead	38	14	9	15	52	54	51
Westfield	38	12	13	13	54	50	49
Thatcham Town	38	12	12	14	56	57	48
Uxbridge	38	11	11	16	53	55	44
Guernsey	38	10	10	18	42	73	40
Ashford Town	38	11	5	22	46	91	38
Sutton Common Rovers	38	10	7	21	45	71	37
Merstham	38	7	15	16	43	66	36
Bedfont Sports	***38***	***7***	***14***	***17***	***50***	***62***	***35***
Tooting & Mitcham United	***38***	***5***	***9***	***24***	***34***	***65***	***24***

Basingstoke Town and Walton & Hersham were both promoted to the Southern League Premier South division.

Isthmian League South East Division 2022/2023 Season	Ashford United	Beckenham Town	Burgess Hill Town	Chatham Town	Chichester City	Corinthian	Cray Valley Paper Mills	East Grinstead Town	Faversham Town	Haywards Heath Town	Hythe Town	Lancing	Littlehampton Town	Ramsgate	Sevenoaks Town	Sheppey United	Sittingbourne	Three Bridges	VCD Athletic	Whitehawk
Ashford United		2-2	3-2	1-4	1-1	0-0	1-0	2-2	3-0	4-0	1-0	1-0	3-2	1-2	1-0	0-1	0-0	2-1	0-1	1-1
Beckenham Town	1-2		2-1	2-0	4-1	3-2	0-0	1-1	2-0	0-0	0-0	4-0	4-2	1-1	4-2	2-1	1-0	3-0	1-2	2-0
Burgess Hill Town	0-1	0-0		0-1	2-2	4-1	0-3	1-0	4-1	1-1	1-4	4-4	0-2	0-1	1-3	1-3	2-1	2-1	1-2	0-1
Chatham Town	1-0	3-0	2-1		2-1	1-0	2-1	1-0	2-0	0-0	6-1	2-1	1-0	2-0	2-1	0-0	1-1	2-2	3-0	2-1
Chichester City	1-0	2-1	1-0	2-4		1-1	0-2	2-0	1-1	4-0	1-0	1-0	3-0	2-2	1-0	0-2	1-1	2-1	2-0	4-1
Corinthian	0-4	0-1	0-1	0-1	2-1		1-2	1-1	0-2	0-3	0-2	0-2	1-1	2-3	0-0	1-1	3-0	0-2	3-2	0-2
Cray Valley Paper Mills	5-1	2-3	3-1	3-1	0-1	0-0		1-0	5-0	5-0	2-0	2-1	2-2	2-0	0-1	2-2	1-3	3-2	2-1	2-2
East Grinstead Town	2-2	0-2	0-4	1-0	3-2	1-0	0-3		1-0	2-1	3-2	2-0	0-1	1-3	3-0	0-1	1-3	1-1	2-2	3-2
Faversham Town	1-0	0-3	2-1	1-2	1-0	1-1	2-0	3-1		2-2	0-1	1-3	2-3	1-3	1-2	2-3	0-1	4-0	0-1	1-1
Haywards Heath Town	0-2	2-1	0-2	2-2	2-2	2-2	1-3	2-0	2-2		2-1	2-2	2-0	1-2	2-5	2-1	0-2	1-1	1-1	1-2
Hythe Town	1-1	3-0	1-0	1-0	1-0	2-1	1-1	4-0	1-0	4-0		3-1	0-0	0-1	0-0	1-0	1-0	1-1	0-0	1-0
Lancing	3-2	2-3	2-3	0-1	1-0	1-0	1-1	0-1	2-1	2-3	2-0		1-0	1-1	3-1	1-2	3-1	3-0	2-1	0-0
Littlehampton Town	1-3	4-1	1-1	1-4	1-1	5-1	1-0	1-1	0-2	3-2	1-4	1-1		2-0	0-1	2-3	1-1	1-0	1-0	0-1
Ramsgate	3-2	1-1	4-1	2-0	0-0	2-0	3-0	5-0	3-3	3-3	2-1	2-1	2-0		2-4	1-2	1-1	4-1	2-1	1-1
Sevenoaks Town	2-1	4-0	1-1	2-3	3-3	0-1	0-3	3-1	2-1	3-1	0-1	3-0	4-0	1-2		0-3	0-0	1-0	2-2	2-1
Sheppey United	2-1	5-1	2-4	2-2	1-1	1-0	1-3	4-1	2-2	2-4	1-0	2-0	7-3	3-3	0-1		0-1	3-2	1-0	1-1
Sittingbourne	1-3	2-3	4-0	0-0	2-1	3-0	0-0	2-0	2-1	5-0	2-3	1-1	0-1	0-0	1-1	1-4		1-1	3-1	0-2
Three Bridges	0-2	1-2	0-0	3-2	2-2	1-2	2-2	2-3	3-1	4-1	1-3	3-0	2-0	2-0	1-3	4-1	2-1		2-0	3-2
VCD Athletic	2-1	0-1	2-2	1-3	3-5	1-4	0-4	3-4	5-0	2-1	1-2	1-0	0-0	2-2	2-1	2-1	0-2	0-0		0-2
Whitehawk	2-2	1-0	0-0	1-0	2-0	1-1	2-0	2-0	6-1	2-1	2-0	4-0	1-3	1-3	3-1	2-0	2-1	3-0	4-0	

Isthmian League South East Division

Season 2022/2023

Chatham Town	**38**	**24**	**7**	**7**	**65**	**35**	**79**
Ramsgate	38	20	12	6	72	47	72
Whitehawk	**38**	**20**	**9**	**9**	**64**	**37**	**69**
Beckenham Town	38	20	8	10	62	49	68
Hythe Town	38	20	7	11	51	34	67
Cray Valley Paper Mills	38	19	9	10	70	39	66
Sheppey United	38	19	8	11	71	54	65
Sevenoaks Town	38	17	7	14	60	51	58
Ashford United	38	16	9	13	57	47	57
Chichester City	38	14	12	12	55	49	54
Sittingbourne	38	13	12	13	50	42	51
Littlehampton Town	38	12	9	17	47	62	45
Lancing	38	12	7	19	47	60	43
East Grinstead Town	38	12	7	19	42	69	43
Three Bridges	38	11	9	18	54	64	42
Burgess Hill Town	38	10	9	19	49	62	39
VCD Athletic	***38***	***10***	***8***	***20***	***44***	***67***	***38***
Haywards Heath Town	***38***	***8***	***12***	***18***	***50***	***81***	***36***
Faversham Town	***38***	***8***	***7***	***23***	***43***	***74***	***31***
Corinthian	***38***	***6***	***10***	***22***	***31***	***61***	***28***

F.A. Trophy 2022/2023

Qualifying 1	AFC Totton	1	Slimbridge	1	(aet)
	AFC Totton won 7-6 on penalties.				
Qualifying 1	Ashford United	3	AFC Sudbury	3	(aet)
	Ashford United won 5-4 on penalties.				
Qualifying 1	Aylesbury United	0	Evesham United	3	
Qualifying 1	Barton Rovers	0	Chatham Town	1	
Qualifying 1	Bashley	4	Frome Town	1	
Qualifying 1	Basildon United	0	Lowestoft Town	2	
Qualifying 1	Basingstoke Town	3	Cirencester Town	5	
Qualifying 1	Beckenham Town	1	Heybridge Swifts	1	(aet)
	Heybridge Swifts won 4-1 on penalties.				
Qualifying 1	Bedfont Sports	2	Hashtag United	2	(aet)
	Bedfont Sports won 5-4 on penalties.				
Qualifying 1	Bedworth United	0	Harborough Town	1	
Qualifying 1	Berkhamsted	5	Exmouth Town	0	
Qualifying 1	Bishop's Cleeve	2	AFC Dunstable	3	
Qualifying 1	Boldmere St. Michaels	4	Sporting Khalsa	3	
Qualifying 1	Bootle		Grimsby Borough		
	Grimsby Borough withdrew so Bootle received a walkover.				
Qualifying 1	Bridlington Town	1	Colne	2	
Qualifying 1	Brighouse Town	0	Worksop Town	2	
Qualifying 1	Bury Town	1	Stowmarket Town	2	
Qualifying 1	Cambridge City	4	Yaxley	1	
Qualifying 1	Carlton Town	2	Hanley Town	0	
Qualifying 1	Chertsey Town	1	Uxbridge	3	
Qualifying 1	Chichester City	0	Faversham Town	1	
Qualifying 1	Chipstead	4	Waltham Abbey	2	
Qualifying 1	Cinderford Town	0	Thatcham Town	1	
Qualifying 1	City of Liverpool	0	Sheffield	0	(aet)
	Sheffield won 4-2 on penalties.				
Qualifying 1	Clitheroe	2	1874 Northwich	1	
Qualifying 1	Coleshill Town	3	St Neots Town	2	
Qualifying 1	Daventry Town	2	Lincoln United	3	
Qualifying 1	Didcot Town	1	Hamworthy United	1	(aet)
	Didcot Town won 5-4 on penalties.				
Qualifying 1	East Thurrock United	3	Sutton Common Rovers	1	
Qualifying 1	FC Romania	1	Westfield (Surrey)	1	(aet)
	FC Romania won 4-2 on penalties.				
Qualifying 1	Felixstowe & Walton United	2	Burgess Hill Town	2	(aet)
	Burgess Hill Town won 3-2 on penalties.				
Qualifying 1	Gorleston	1	Coggeshall Town	1	(aet)
	Coggeshall Town won 7-6 on penalties.				
Qualifying 1	Grantham Town	1	Sutton Coldfield Town	2	
Qualifying 1	Great Wakering Rovers	1	Harlow Town	2	
Qualifying 1	Hadley	1	Sevenoaks Town	2	
Qualifying 1	Halesowen Town	5	Biggleswade	2	
Qualifying 1	Haywards Heath Town	0	Southall	0	(aet)
	Southall won 8-7 on penalties.				
Qualifying 1	Highworth Town	1	Paulton Rovers	2	
Qualifying 1	Kempston Rovers	0	Dereham Town	1	
Qualifying 1	Kidlington	0	Tavistock	0	(aet)
	Tavistock won 4-2 on penalties.				
Qualifying 1	Kidsgrove Athletic	3	Hinckley LR	4	
Qualifying 1	Lancing	1	Cray Valley Paper Mills	4	
Qualifying 1	Larkhall Athletic	0	Melksham Town	2	

Qualifying 1	Littlehampton Town	1	Ramsgate	0	
Qualifying 1	Long Eaton United	2	Gresley Rovers	0	
Qualifying 1	Loughborough Dynamo	3	Corby Town	1	
Qualifying 1	Macclesfield	7	Tadcaster Albion	0	
Qualifying 1	Maldon & Tiptree	0	Ware	3	
Qualifying 1	Marlow	0	Binfield	4	
Qualifying 1	Merstham	3	Hythe Town	0	
Qualifying 1	Mossley	1	Dunston	2	
Qualifying 1	Newcastle Town	0	Spalding United	2	
Qualifying 1	North Shields	3	Pontefract Collieries	1	
Qualifying 1	Northwood	0	Hanworth Villa	3	
Qualifying 1	Prescot Cables	1	Cleethorpes Town	1	(aet)
	Prescot Cables won 4-2 on penalties.				
Qualifying 1	Ramsbottom United	2	Glossop North End	1	
Qualifying 1	Sheppey United	3	Hertford Town	3	(aet)
	Hertford Town won 3-2 on penalties.				
Qualifying 1	Shepshed Dynamo	1	Biggleswade Town	0	
Qualifying 1	Shildon	1	Consett	2	
Qualifying 1	Sholing	0	Lymington Town	1	
Qualifying 1	South Park	1	Sittingbourne	2	
Qualifying 1	Stamford	1	Chasetown	2	
Qualifying 1	Stocksbridge Park Steels	2	Ossett United	2	(aet)
	Ossett United won 3-0 on penalties.				
Qualifying 1	Thame United	2	Westbury United	0	
Qualifying 1	Three Bridges	3	Hullbridge Sports	2	
Qualifying 1	Tilbury	1	Whitehawk	2	
Qualifying 1	Tooting & Mitcham United	0	Corinthian	0	(aet)
	Corinthian won 7-6 on penalties.				
Qualifying 1	Trafford	1	Hebburn Town	2	
Qualifying 1	VCD Athletic	0	Grays Athletic	3	
Qualifying 1	Walthamstow	1	Ashford Town (Middlesex)	3	
Qualifying 1	Walton & Hersham	3	Leatherhead	1	
Qualifying 1	Welwyn Garden City	1	New Salamis	2	
Qualifying 1	Widnes	1	Skelmersdale United	1	(aet)
	Widnes won 4-2 on penalties.				
Qualifying 1	Willand Rovers	0	Bideford	3	
Qualifying 1	Wimborne Town	2	Bristol Manor Farm	3	
Qualifying 1	Witham Town	1	Brentwood Town	0	
Qualifying 1	Witton Albion	3	Stockton Town	4	
Qualifying 1	Workington	1	Runcorn Linnets	2	
Qualifying 1	Wroxham	4	East Grinstead Town	1	
Qualifying 2	AFC Totton	2	Berkhamsted	1	
Qualifying 2	Ashford United	2	Three Bridges	0	
Qualifying 2	Bashley	2	Melksham Town	2	(aet)
	Melksham Town won 5-4 on penalties.				
Qualifying 2	Boldmere St. Michaels	1	Chasetown	1	(aet)
	Chasetown won 5-4 on penalties.				
Qualifying 2	Bootle	0	Dunston	3	
Qualifying 2	Bristol Manor Farm	2	Bideford	2	(aet)
	Bristol Manor Farm won 5-4 on penalties.				
Qualifying 2	Chatham Town	0	Stowmarket Town	1	
Qualifying 2	Cirencester Town	3	Paulton Rovers	2	
Qualifying 2	Coleshill Town	4	Leek Town	4	(aet)
	Leek Town won 4-2 on penalties.				
Qualifying 2	Colne	1	Consett	0	
Qualifying 2	Corinthian	2	Whitehawk	4	

Round	Home		Away		
Qualifying 2	Cray Valley Paper Mills	5	East Thurrock United	3	
Qualifying 2	Dereham Town	0	Spalding United	1	
Qualifying 2	Evesham United	1	Lymington Town	0	
Qualifying 2	FC Romania	2	Faversham Town	3	
Qualifying 2	Grays Athletic	4	Merstham	1	
Qualifying 2	Hanworth Villa	3	Littlehampton Town	2	
Qualifying 2	Harborough Town	2	Shepshed Dynamo	1	
Qualifying 2	Harlow Town	4	Ashford Town (Middlesex)	1	
Qualifying 2	Hebburn Town	3	Stockton Town	1	
Qualifying 2	Heybridge Swifts	2	Chipstead	1	
Qualifying 2	Hinckley LR	0	Cambridge City	0	(aet)
	Hinckley LR won 3-0 on penalties.				
Qualifying 2	Lincoln United	1	Carlton Town	1	(aet)
	Lincoln United won 4-3 on penalties.				
Qualifying 2	Long Eaton United	0	Loughborough Dynamo	0	(aet)
	Loughborough Dynamo won 4-2 on penalties.				
Qualifying 2	Macclesfield	5	Widnes	1	
Qualifying 2	New Salamis	3	Coggeshall Town	0	
Qualifying 2	North Shields	1	Runcorn Linnets	2	
Qualifying 2	Prescot Cables	1	Worksop Town	3	
Qualifying 2	Ramsbottom United	1	Clitheroe	4	
Qualifying 2	Sevenoaks Town	2	Hertford Town	2	(aet)
	Sevenoaks Town won 5-3 on penalties.				
Qualifying 2	Sheffield	1	Ossett United	1	(aet)
	Ossett United won 4-2 on penalties.				
Qualifying 2	Sittingbourne	1	Burgess Hill Town	1	(aet)
	Burgess Hill Town won 4-3 on penalties.				
Qualifying 2	Sutton Coldfield Town	2	Halesowen Town	0	
Qualifying 2	Tavistock	1	Didcot Town	0	
Qualifying 2	Thame United	1	Binfield	2	
Qualifying 2	Thatcham Town	0	AFC Dunstable	3	
Qualifying 2	Uxbridge	2	Bedfont Sports	0	
Qualifying 2	Walton & Hersham	4	Southall	0	
Qualifying 2	Witham Town	2	Ware	1	
Qualifying 2	Wroxham	5	Lowestoft Town	1	
Qualifying 3	AFC Rushden & Diamonds	0	Tamworth	4	
Qualifying 3	Ashford United	1	Kings Langley	2	
Qualifying 3	Ashton United	0	Dunston	0	(aet)
	Dunston won 3-1 on penalties.				
Qualifying 3	Atherton Collieries	0	Leek Town	3	
Qualifying 3	Basford United	1	Harborough Town	1	(aet)
	Basford United won 5-3 on penalties.				
Qualifying 3	Beaconsfield Town	2	Hartley Wintney	2	(aet)
	Beaconsfield Town won 3-1 on penalties.				
Qualifying 3	Bedford Town	0	Alvechurch	3	
Qualifying 3	Belper Town	1	St Ives Town	1	(aet)
	Belper Town won 4-2 on penalties.				
Qualifying 3	Billericay Town	2	Margate	0	
Qualifying 3	Bognor Regis Town	1	Bowers & Pitsea	0	
Qualifying 3	Bristol Manor Farm	2	Gosport Borough	0	
Qualifying 3	Bromsgrove Sporting	0	Chasetown	3	
Qualifying 3	Burgess Hill Town	2	Hanworth Villa	1	
Qualifying 3	Canvey Island	1	Bracknell Town	4	
Qualifying 3	Carshalton Athletic	2	Cray Valley Paper Mills	2	(aet)
	Carshalton Athletic won 4-3 on penalties.				

Round	Home		Away		
Qualifying 3	Clitheroe	2	Marske United	2	(aet)
	Marske United won 4-1 on penalties.				
Qualifying 3	Coalville Town	4	Ilkeston Town (3)	1	
Qualifying 3	Corinthian Casuals	2	Harrow Borough	2	(aet)
	Harrow Borough won 3-1 on penalties.				
Qualifying 3	Enfield Town	0	Chesham United	4	
Qualifying 3	FC United of Manchester	0	Liversedge	1	
Qualifying 3	Folkestone Invicta	1	Whitehawk	1	(aet)
	Folkestone Invicta won 4-3 on penalties.				
Qualifying 3	Gainsborough Trinity	3	Barwell	1	
Qualifying 3	Grays Athletic	0	Faversham Town	0	(aet)
	Grays Athletic won 4-2 on penalties.				
Qualifying 3	Guiseley	3	Whitby Town	1	
Qualifying 3	Hanwell Town	3	Cray Wanderers	1	
Qualifying 3	Haringey Borough	1	Brightlingsea Regent	0	
Qualifying 3	Harlow Town	2	Hornchurch	2	(aet)
	Harlow Town won 3-1 on penalties.				
Qualifying 3	Hayes & Yeading United	1	New Salamis	0	
Qualifying 3	Hebburn Town	1	Warrington Town	2	
Qualifying 3	Hendon	0	Binfield	0	(aet)
	Binfield won 5-4 on penalties.				
Qualifying 3	Herne Bay	1	Bishop's Stortford	2	
Qualifying 3	Hitchin Town	0	Redditch United	3	
Qualifying 3	Horsham	4	Aveley	3	
Qualifying 3	Hyde United	2	Colne	3	
Qualifying 3	Kingstonian	2	Wingate & Finchley	2	(aet)
	Wingate & Finchley won 4-2 on penalties.				
Qualifying 3	Leiston	1	Evesham United	0	
Qualifying 3	Lewes	1	Sevenoaks Town	0	
Qualifying 3	Lincoln United	1	Wroxham	3	
Qualifying 3	Loughborough Dynamo	1	Worksop Town	2	
Qualifying 3	Macclesfield	6	Bamber Bridge	1	
Qualifying 3	Marine	1	Radcliffe	1	(aet)
	Marine won 4-3 on penalties.				
Qualifying 3	Matlock Town	3	Sutton Coldfield Town	0	
Qualifying 3	Merthyr Town	0	AFC Totton	1	
Qualifying 3	Metropolitan Police	0	Hastings United	0	(aet)
	Hastings United won 5-4 on penalties.				
Qualifying 3	Morpeth Town	2	Lancaster City	3	
Qualifying 3	Nantwich Town	0	Warrington Rylands	2	
Qualifying 3	Needham Market	0	Stourbridge	1	
Qualifying 3	North Leigh	3	Tiverton Town	3	(aet)
	North Leigh won 5-3 on penalties.				
Qualifying 3	Nuneaton Borough	2	Hinckley LR	0	
Qualifying 3	Plymouth Parkway	2	Dorchester Town	0	
Qualifying 3	Potters Bar Town	0	Heybridge Swifts	2	
Qualifying 3	Runcorn Linnets	2	Ossett United	1	
Qualifying 3	Rushall Olympic	3	Hednesford Town	4	
Qualifying 3	Spalding United	1	Stafford Rangers	2	
Qualifying 3	Stalybridge Celtic	1	South Shields	2	
Qualifying 3	Stowmarket Town	1	Mickleover	1	(aet)
	Stowmarket Town won 3-0 on penalties.				
Qualifying 3	Stratford Town	1	Royston Town	2	
Qualifying 3	Swindon Supermarine	3	Cirencester Town	0	
Qualifying 3	Tavistock	3	Melksham Town	1	
Qualifying 3	Truro City	1	Salisbury	0	

Qualifying 3	Uxbridge	1	Walton & Hersham	0	
Qualifying 3	Winchester City	2	Poole Town	0	
Qualifying 3	Witham Town	0	AFC Dunstable	1	
Qualifying 3	Yate Town	0	Weston-Super-Mare	2	
Round 1	AFC Dunstable	0	Hanwell Town	1	
Round 1	Basford United	1	Marine	2	
Round 1	Beaconsfield Town	2	Truro City	0	
Round 1	Bracknell Town	3	North Leigh	2	
Round 1	Carshalton Athletic	0	Kings Langley	1	
Round 1	Chasetown	0	Marske United	2	
Round 1	Chesham United	2	Lewes	2	(aet)
	Lewes won 3-1 on penalties.				
Round 1	Colne	5	Warrington Rylands	0	
Round 1	Dunston	1	Coalville Town	3	
Round 1	Folkestone Invicta	2	Horsham	0	
Round 1	Grays Athletic	0	Stowmarket Town	1	
Round 1	Haringey Borough	1	Billericay Town	3	
Round 1	Harlow Town	0	Bishop's Stortford	4	
Round 1	Harrow Borough	2	Hayes & Yeading United	0	
Round 1	Hastings United	4	Burgess Hill Town	2	
Round 1	Hednesford Town	4	Stourbridge	2	
Round 1	Lancaster City	3	Gainsborough Trinity	2	
Round 1	Leek Town	2	Worksop Town	1	
Round 1	Leiston	2	Wroxham	1	
Round 1	Liversedge	0	Tamworth	2	
Round 1	Macclesfield	0	Guiseley	2	
Round 1	Matlock Town	1	Stafford Rangers	0	
Round 1	Nuneaton Borough	1	Alvechurch	2	
Round 1	Plymouth Parkway	3	Bristol Manor Farm	1	
Round 1	Redditch United	3	AFC Totton	1	
Round 1	Royston Town	0	Heybridge Swifts	2	
Round 1	Runcorn Linnets	3	Belper Town	2	
Round 1	Tavistock	2	Binfield	1	
Round 1	Uxbridge	4	Wingate & Finchley	2	
Round 1	Warrington Town	3	South Shields	1	
Round 1	Weston-Super-Mare	1	Bognor Regis Town	2	
Round 1	Winchester City	0	Swindon Supermarine	5	
Round 2	AFC Fylde	2	Colne	1	
Round 2	Banbury United	6	Stowmarket Town	0	
Round 2	Beaconsfield Town	1	Folkestone Invicta	1	(aet)
	Folkestone Invicta won 5-4 on penalties.				
Round 2	Billericay Town	1	Bath City	3	
Round 2	Blyth Spartans	4	Buxton	2	
Round 2	Bradford Park Avenue	1	Farsley Celtic FC	2	
Round 2	Braintree Town	1	Brackley Town	0	
Round 2	Chelmsford City	2	Redditch United	1	
Round 2	Chester FC	2	Lancaster City	1	
Round 2	Chorley	1	Leek Town	0	
Round 2	Coalville Town	2	Hednesford Town	0	
Round 2	Concord Rangers	2	Harrow Borough	4	
Round 2	Darlington	4	Alfreton Town	1	
Round 2	Ebbsfleet United	0	Eastbourne Borough	1	
Round 2	Hampton & Richmond Borough	0	Farnborough	1	
Round 2	Hanwell Town	0	Slough Town	3	
Round 2	Hastings United	1	Chippenham Town	2	
Round 2	Heybridge Swifts	3	Hereford	0	
Round 2	Kettering Town	1	Gloucester City	0	
	Kettering Town were subsequently disqualified after fielding an ineligible player.				

Round 2	King's Lynn Town	1	Hemel Hempstead Town	1	(aet)
	Hemel Hempstead Town won 5-4 on penalties.				
Round 2	Kings Langley	1	AFC Telford United	2	
Round 2	Leamington	1	Bishop's Stortford	0	
Round 2	Leiston	4	Alvechurch	3	
Round 2	Lewes	2	Bognor Regis Town	2	(aet)
	Bognor Regis Town won 4-2 on penalties.				
Round 2	Marine	1	Scarborough Athletic	0	
Round 2	Matlock Town	1	Marske United	2	
Round 2	Oxford City	1	Plymouth Parkway	1	(aet)
	Plymouth Parkway won 4-2 on penalties.				
Round 2	Peterborough Sports	3	Cheshunt	2	
Round 2	Southport	1	Curzon Ashton	3	
Round 2	Spennymoor Town	3	Runcorn Linnets	2	
Round 2	St Albans City	1	Kidderminster Harriers	2	
Round 2	Swindon Supermarine	4	Dartford	0	
Round 2	Tamworth	1	Boston United	1	(aet)
	Tamworth won 3-2 on penalties.				
Round 2	Taunton Town	2	Dulwich Hamlet	1	
Round 2	Tavistock	1	Hungerford Town	2	
Round 2	Tonbridge Angels	2	Bracknell Town	4	
Round 2	Uxbridge	1	Dover Athletic	1	(aet)
	Uxbridge won 4-2 on penalties.				
Round 2	Warrington Town	0	Guiseley	1	
Round 2	Welling United	3	Havant & Waterlooville	2	
Round 2	Worthing	4	Weymouth	2	
Round 3	AFC Fylde	1	Kidderminster Harriers	1	(aet)
	Kidderminster Harriers won 4-2 on penalties.				
Round 3	Aldershot Town	3	Welling United	0	
Round 3	Altrincham	1	Curzon Ashton	0	
Round 3	Banbury United	4	Bognor Regis Town	3	
Round 3	Barnet	1	Plymouth Parkway	0	
Round 3	Bath City	2	Bromley	2	(aet)
	Bath City won 5-4 on penalties.				
Round 3	Chelmsford City	2	Wealdstone	1	
Round 3	Chesterfield	1	Coalville Town	3	
Round 3	Dagenham & Redbridge	5	Uxbridge	1	
Round 3	Eastbourne Borough	1	Bracknell Town	2	
Round 3	Farnborough	2	Braintree Town	2	(aet)
	Braintree Town won 5-4 on penalties.				
Round 3	Farsley Celtic FC	2	Chester FC	2	(aet)
	Farsley Celtic won 5-4 on penalties.				
Round 3	Folkestone Invicta	1	Leiston	1	(aet)
	Leiston won 4-1 on penalties.				
Round 3	Gateshead	5	Gloucester City	1	
Round 3	Guiseley	0	FC Halifax Town	1	
Round 3	Hemel Hempstead Town	2	Maidenhead United	3	
Round 3	Heybridge Swifts	1	Hungerford Town	1	(aet)
	Hungerford Town won 5-3 on penalties.				
Round 3	Maidstone United (2)	2	Worthing	0	
Round 3	Marske United	2	Marine	1	
Round 3	Notts County	2	Chorley	1	
Round 3	Oldham Athletic	0	Peterborough Sports	0	(aet)
	Oldham Athletic won 3-2 on penalties.				
Round 3	Slough Town	0	Taunton Town	1	
Round 3	Solihull Moors	2	AFC Telford United	0	
Round 3	Southend United	2	Boreham Wood	0	
Round 3	Spennymoor Town	1	Darlington	3	

Round 3	Swindon Supermarine	1	Harrow Borough	2	
Round 3	Tamworth	2	Leamington	1	
Round 3	Torquay United	3	Chippenham Town	2	
Round 3	Woking	0	Eastleigh	2	
Round 3	Wrexham	3	Scunthorpe United	1	
Round 3	Yeovil Town	0	Dorking Wanderers	0	(aet)
	Dorking Wanderers won 4-1 on penalties.				
Round 3	York City	5	Blyth Spartans	0	
Round 4	Aldershot Town	4	Leiston	1	
Round 4	Altrincham	2	Wrexham	2	(aet)
	Altrincham won 4-3 on penalties.				
Round 4	Banbury United	3	Coalville Town	2	
Round 4	Bracknell Town	1	Bath City	0	
Round 4	Dagenham & Redbridge	0	Maidenhead United	2	
Round 4	Dorking Wanderers	3	Kidderminster Harriers	2	
Round 4	Eastleigh	1	Braintree Town	0	
Round 4	Farsley Celtic FC	7	Marske United	1	
Round 4	Gateshead	3	Oldham Athletic	1	
Round 4	Harrow Borough	2	FC Halifax Town	2	(aet)
	FC Halifax Town won 6-5 on penalties.				
Round 4	Hungerford Town	2	Tamworth	1	
Round 4	Notts County	2	Maidstone United	2	(aet)
	Maidstone United won 6-5 on penalties.				
Round 4	Solihull Moors	0	Barnet	2	
Round 4	Southend United	2	Darlington	1	
Round 4	Torquay United	4	Taunton Town	2	
Round 4	York City	1	Chelmsford City	1	(aet)
	York City won 5-4 on penalties.				
Round 5	Aldershot Town	1	Dorking Wanderers	0	
Round 5	Banbury United	0	Gateshead	1	
Round 5	Bracknell Town	1	Altrincham	3	
Round 5	Eastleigh	0	Maidstone United	4	
Round 5	Hungerford Town	2	Farsley Celtic FC	3	
Round 5	Maidenhead United	0	FC Halifax Town	0	(aet)
	FC Halifax Town won 5-4 on penalties.				
Round 5	Southend United	0	York City	2	
Round 5	Torquay United	1	Barnet	2	
Round 6	Aldershot Town	0	FC Halifax Town	2	
Round 6	Gateshead	0	Farsley Celtic FC	0	(aet)
	Gateshead won 4-2 on penalties.				
Round 6	Maidstone United	2	Barnet	2	(aet)
	Barnet won 4-3 on penalties.				
Round 6	York City	1	Altrincham	2	
Semi-final	Altrincham	1	FC Halifax Town	1	(aet)
	FC Halifax Town won 3-2 on penalties.				
Semi-final	Gateshead	3	Barnet	3	(aet)
	Gateshead won 4-1 on penalties.				
FINAL	FC Halifax Town	1	Gateshead	0	

F.A. Vase 2022/2023

Round 1	AFC Darwen	3	Charnock Richard	2	
Round 1	AFC Portchester	2	Phoenix Sports	3	
Round 1	AFC Stoneham	3	Fisher	3	
Round 1	AFC Whyteleafe	7	Snodland Town	1	
Round 1	Baldock Town	2	Benfleet	2	(aet)
	Baldock Town won 4-3 on penalties.				
Round 1	Barnoldswick Town	5	Selby Town	4	
Round 1	Barton Town	2	Cheadle Town	4	
Round 1	Bedfont (2)	1	Redhill	0	
Round 1	Biggleswade United	2	Redbridge	0	
Round 1	Billingham Town	1	FC Isle of Man	4	
Round 1	Birstall United	0	AFC Wulfrunians	1	
Round 1	Bishops Lydeard	1	Roman Glass St George	2	
Round 1	Blackstones	1	Bournemouth (Ams)	1	(aet)
	Blackstones won 3-1 on penalties.				
Round 1	Bovey Tracey	1	Ivybridge Town	1	(aet)
	Bovey Tracey won 4-3 on penalties.				
Round 1	Bradford Town	0	Laverstock & Ford	3	
Round 1	Brandon United	2	Thackley	3	
Round 1	Bridport	3	Royal Wootton Bassett Town	5	
Round 1	Brigg Town	2	Harrogate Railway Athletic	0	
Round 1	Brimscombe & Thrupp	1	Torpoint Athletic	1	(aet)
	Brimscombe & Thrupp won 5-4 on penalties.				
Round 1	British Airways	1	Abbey Rangers	1	(aet)
	Abbey Rangers won 4-2 on penalties.				
Round 1	Brixham AFC	4	Odd Down	0	
Round 1	Brocton	1	Wolverhampton Casuals	1	
	Wolverhampton Casuals were disqualified after fielding an ineligible player.				
Round 1	Buckhurst Hill	2	Basildon Town	2	(aet)
	Buckhurst Hill won 5-3 on penalties.				
Round 1	Burnham Ramblers	0	Ely City	0	(aet)
	Burnham Ramblers won 4-2 on penalties.				
Round 1	Bury AFC	3	Bishop Auckland	0	
Round 1	Campion	1	Bacup Borough	3	
Round 1	Cheltenham Saracens	3	Belper United	5	
Round 1	Chessington & Hook United	4	Berks County	1	
Round 1	Coventry United	3	Romulus	3	(aet)
	Coventry United won 3-1 on penalties.				
Round 1	Cribbs	4	Portland United	2	
Round 1	Crowborough Athletic	4	Eversley & California	1	
Round 1	Cullompton Rangers	2	Bemerton Heath Harlequins	0	
Round 1	Deal Town	7	Tooting Bec	0	
Round 1	Downham Town	2	Stansted	3	
Round 1	Dunstable Town	2	Norwich CBS	1	
Round 1	Eastbourne Town	6	Brook House	0	
Round 1	Elburton Villa	1	Ashton & Backwell United	0	
Round 1	Erith Town	1	Crawley Down Gatwick	0	
Round 1	FC St Helens	2	Penistone Church	1	
Round 1	Falmouth Town	2	Helston Athletic	1	
Round 1	Fleet Town	1	Colliers Wood United	2	
Round 1	Frickley Athletic	1	Emley	3	
Round 1	Frimley Green	0	North Greenford United	7	
Round 1	Godmanchester Rovers	1	Little Oakley	2	
Round 1	Harpenden Town	2	St Panteleimon	3	
Round 1	Hartpury University	1	Tuffley Rovers	0	
Round 1	Hinckley	4	Cogenhoe United	1	

Round 1	Holker Old Boys	3	Whickham	1	
Round 1	Horden CW	3	Armthorpe Welfare	0	
Round 1	Horndean	1	Bexhill United	2	
Round 1	Jersey Bulls	3	Bearsted	1	
Round 1	Kendal Town	3	Longridge Town	4	
Round 1	Kennington	3	Blackfield & Langley	1	
Round 1	Keynsham Town	0	Corsham Town	4	
Round 1	Larkfield & New Hythe	3	Edgware & Kingsbury	1	
Round 1	Little Common	3	Milton United (Oxon)	1	
Round 1	London Samurai Rovers	3	Wallingford & Crowmarsh	4	
Round 1	Lydd Town	0	Holyport	0	(aet)
	Holyport won 5-4 on penalties.				
Round 1	Lydney Town	1	Mousehole	3	
Round 1	Lye Town	8	Northampton Sileby Rangers	0	
Round 1	Mangotsfield United	2	Crediton United	0	
Round 1	May & Baker Eastbrook Community	1	Enfield	3	
Round 1	Newark & Sherwood United	3	Ashby Ivanhoe	0	
Round 1	Newcastle Benfield	4	Newton Aycliffe	0	
Round 1	Newcastle University	2	Hallam	5	
Round 1	Newent Town	1	Eccleshall	1	(aet)
	Eccleshall won 5-3 on penalties.				
Round 1	Newmarket Town	3	Romford	4	
Round 1	Newport (IOW)	0	Ascot United	1	
Round 1	Norwich United	3	Barkingside	1	
Round 1	Oldland Abbotonians	0	Shaftesbury	0	(aet)
	Shaftesbury won 4-3 on penalties.				
Round 1	Oxhey Jets	3	Wisbech Town	1	
Round 1	Pagham	0	Sporting Bengal United	1	
Round 1	Peacehaven & Telscombe	4	Horley Town	0	
Round 1	Pershore Town	1	Atherstone Town	2	
Round 1	Quorn	1	Highgate United	3	
Round 1	Racing Club Warwick	1	Dunkirk	2	
Round 1	Rayners Lane	1	Cowes Sports	2	
Round 1	Rising Ballers Kensington	0	Harefield United	5	
Round 1	Rusthall	2	Montpelier Villa	2	(aet)
	Montpelier Villa won 5-4 on penalties.				
Round 1	Sandbach United	2	Kimberley MW	0	
Round 1	Seaham Red Star	1	Eccleshill United	2	
Round 1	Shefford Town & Campton	1	Leighton Town	1	(aet)
	Leighton Town won 3-1 on penalties.				
Round 1	Sherwood Colliery	3	Pinchbeck United	4	
Round 1	Squires Gate	2	Cammell Laird 1907	1	
Round 1	St Blazey	1	Thornbury Town	2	
Round 1	Stapenhill	1	Walsall Wood	6	
Round 1	Stone Old Alleynians	3	Shirebrook Town	2	
Round 1	Stourport Swifts	4	Shifnal Town	2	
Round 1	Street	1	Andover New Street	5	
Round 1	Tadley Calleva	1	Guildford City	1	(aet)
	Guildford City won 4-2 on penalties.				
Round 1	Thornaby	2	Pilkington	2	(aet)
	Thornaby won 5-4 on penalties.				
Round 1	Tividale	1	Radford	[illegible]	(aet)
	Tividale				
Round 1	Tring Athletic	3	Aylesbury Vale Dynamos	2	
Round 1	Wellington (Somerset)	2	Barnstaple Town	0	
Round 1	West Didsbury & Chorlton	2	Golcar United	1	
Round 1	Westfields	0	Ollerton Town	1	
Round 1	Whitchurch United	0	Broadbridge Heath	5	
Round 1	Whitley Bay	4	Billingham Synthonia	2	

Round 1	Whittlesey Athletic	2	Diss Town	2	(aet)
	Whittlesey Athletic won 4-3 on penalties.				
Round 1	Winterton Rangers	1	Prestwich Heys	2	
Round 1	Woodford Town	3	Sawbridgeworth Town	3	(aet)
	Woodford Town won 4-2 on penalties.				
Round 1	Worcester City	0	Wellingborough Town (2)	1	
Round 1	Wormley Rovers	1	Sheringham	1	(aet)
	Sheringham won 4-2 on penalties.				
Round 2	AFC Darwen	2	Thornaby	1	
Round 2	AFC Liverpool	1	FC St Helens	1	(aet)
	AFC Liverpool won 4-3 on penalties.				
Round 2	Anstey Nomads	3	Wellingborough Town (2)	0	
Round 2	Atherstone Town	2	Stone Old Alleynians	0	
Round 2	Athletic Newham	4	Kennington	0	
Round 2	Bacup Borough	2	West Didsbury & Chorlton	2	(aet)
	West Didsbury & Chorlton won 4-1 on penalties.				
Round 2	Baldock Town	1	Newport Pagnell Town	4	
Round 2	Barnoldswick Town	1	Horden CW	2	
Round 2	Belper United	4	Hinckley	1	
Round 2	Bexhill United	0	Eastbourne Town	1	
Round 2	Biggleswade United	3	London Lions	0	
Round 2	Bovey Tracey	4	Brockenhurst	3	
Round 2	Brigg Town	0	Cheadle Town	3	
Round 2	Brimscombe & Thrupp	3	Shaftesbury	3	(aet)
	Shaftesbury won 4-1 on penalties.				
Round 2	Brixham AFC	2	Andover New Street	1	
Round 2	Broadbridge Heath	0	Ascot United	3	
Round 2	Brocton	1	Whitchurch Alport	0	
Round 2	Buckland Athletic	5	Cullompton Rangers	1	
Round 2	Chessington & Hook United	0	Harefield United	3	
Round 2	Clevedon Town	4	Mangotsfield United	0	
Round 2	Colliers Wood United	0	Raynes Park Vale	1	
Round 2	Congleton Town	2	Coventry United	1	
Round 2	Dunstable Town	1	Enfield	0	
Round 2	Eccleshall	0	Coventry Sphinx	3	
Round 2	Egham Town	2	Abbey Rangers	1	
Round 2	Elburton Villa	0	Bridgwater United	4	
Round 2	Emley	1	Squires Gate	1	(aet)
	Squires Gate won 4-2 on penalties.				
Round 2	Erith Town	1	Guildford City (2)	0	
Round 2	Fisher	1	Jersey Bulls	2	
Round 2	Glebe	3	Sporting Bengal United	6	
Round 2	Hallam	1	Bury AFC	1	(aet)
	Bury AFC won 4-1 on penalties.				
Round 2	Holker Old Boys	3	FC Isle of Man	1	
Round 2	Lakenheath	3	Buckhurst Hill	2	
Round 2	Larkfield & New Hythe	2	Tunbridge Wells	0	
Round 2	Laverstock & Ford	2	Falmouth Town	1	
Round 2	Lye Town	4	Ollerton Town	0	
Round 2	Montpelier Villa	0	Holyport	7	
Round 2	Mousehole	1	Hartpury University	2	
Round 2	New Milton Town	2	Cowes Sports	1	
Round 2	Newark & Sherwood United	2	Blackstones	1	
Round 2	Newcastle Benfield	1	Longridge Town	1	(aet)
	Longridge Town won 3-1 on penalties.				
Round 2	North Greenford United	3	AFC Whyteleafe	2	
Round 2	Norwich United	2	Stansted	0	
Round 2	Peacehaven & Telscombe	3	Bedfont	1	

Round 2	Phoenix Sports	2	Deal Town	4	
Round 2	Pinchbeck United	3	Dunkirk	2	
Round 2	Prestwich Heys	1	Whitley Bay	1	(aet)
	Prestwich Heys initially won 8-7 on penalties, but were subsequently disqualified after it was discovered they had fielded an ineligible player.				
Round 2	Roman Glass St George	1	Corsham Town	3	
Round 2	Romford	2	Little Oakley	0	
Round 2	Rugby Town	1	AFC Wulfrunians	2	
Round 2	Saffron Walden Town	0	Leighton Town	2	
Round 2	St. Panteleimon	3	Sheringham	3	(aet)
	St. Panteleimon won 3-2 on penalties.				
Round 2	Stansfeld	2	Crowborough Athletic	1	
Round 2	Stourport Swifts	2	Loughborough Students	1	
Round 2	Thackley	0	Abbey Hey	3	
Round 2	Thornbury Town	1	Cribbs	2	
Round 2	Tividale	0	Highgate United	3	
Round 2	Tring Athletic	1	Burnham Ramblers	1	(aet)
	Tring Athletic won 5-3 on penalties.				
Round 2	Wallingford & Crowmarsh	1	Little Common	4	
Round 2	Walsall Wood	4	Sandbach United	0	
Round 2	Wellington (Somerset)	2	Royal Wootton Bassett Town	2	(aet)
	Royal Wootton Bassett Town won 5-4 on penalties.				
Round 2	Whittlesey Athletic	1	Oxhey Jets	0	
Round 2	Woodford Town	2	Fakenham Town	2	(aet)
	Fakenham Town won 4-3 on penalties.				
Round 2	Wythenshawe Town	2	Eccleshill United	2	(aet)
	Eccleshill United won 4-3 on penalties.				
Round 3	AFC Liverpool	2	Cheadle Town	1	
Round 3	AFC Wulfrunians	3	Brocton	0	
Round 3	Ascot United	4	Little Common	0	
Round 3	Atherstone Town	1	Stourport Swifts	1	(aet)
	Atherstone Town won 4-2 on penalties.				
Round 3	Belper United	0	Coventry Sphinx	6	
Round 3	Biggleswade United	1	Lakenheath	1	(aet)
	Biggleswade United won 3-1 on penalties.				
Round 3	Bridgwater United	1	Cribbs	0	
Round 3	Buckland Athletic	3	Laverstock & Ford	0	
Round 3	Bury AFC	2	Abbey Hey	0	
Round 3	Clevedon Town	1	New Milton Town	1	(aet)
	Clevedon Town won 5-3 on penalties.				
Round 3	Congleton Town	4	Lye Town	3	
Round 3	Dunstable Town	2	Tring Athletic	3	
Round 3	Eastbourne Town	0	Egham Town	1	
Round 3	Harefield United	2	North Greenford United	1	
Round 3	Hartpury University	7	Bovey Tracey	0	
Round 3	Highgate United	0	Walsall Wood	7	
Round 3	Holker Old Boys	4	Squires Gate	2	
Round 3	Holyport	0	Peacehaven & Telscombe	0	(aet)
	Peacehaven & Telscombe won 3-2 on penalties.				
Round 3	Horden CW	2	AFC Darwen	0	
Round 3	Jersey Bulls	5	Athletic Newham	1	
Round 3	Larkfield & New Hythe	1	Raynes Park Vale	2	
Round 3	Leighton Town	2	Fakenham Town	1	
Round 3	Longridge Town	1	Eccleshill United	1	(aet)
	Eccleshill United won 4-2 on penalties.				
Round 3	Newark & Sherwood United	0	Anstey Nomads	2	
Round 3	Norwich United	0	Newport Pagnell Town	1	

Round 3	Pinchbeck United	1	St Panteleimon	0	
Round 3	Royal Wootton Bassett Town	0	Corsham Town	0	(aet)
	Corsham Town won 4-3 on penalties.				
Round 3	Shaftesbury	1	Brixham AFC	1	(aet)
	Brixham AFC won 5-4 on penalties.				
Round 3	Sporting Bengal United	2	Deal Town	2	(aet)
	Deal Town won 5-4 on penalties.				
Round 3	Stansfeld	1	Erith Town	2	
Round 3	Whitley Bay	1	West Didsbury & Chorlton	1	(aet)
	West Didsbury & Chorlton won 4-1 on penalties.				
Round 3	Whittlesey Athletic	1	Romford	3	
Round 4	AFC Wulfrunians	1	Anstey Nomads	0	
Round 4	Atherstone Town	2	Hartpury University	0	
Round 4	Biggleswade United	1	Coventry Sphinx	5	
Round 4	Bridgwater United	0	Erith Town	0	(aet)
	Bridgwater United won 4-1 on penalties.				
Round 4	Brixham AFC	2	Raynes Park Vale	0	
Round 4	Buckland Athletic	1	Ascot United	3	
Round 4	Bury AFC	4	Holker Old Boys	0	
Round 4	Clevedon Town	2	Harefield United	2	(aet)
	Harefield United won 3-1 on penalties.				
Round 4	Congleton Town	4	Pinchbeck United	0	
Round 4	Corsham Town	1	Deal Town	0	
Round 4	Eccleshill United	0	AFC Liverpool	0	(aet)
	Eccleshill United won 5-4 on penalties.				
Round 4	Egham Town	0	Peacehaven & Telscombe	2	
Round 4	Jersey Bulls	6	Romford	0	
Round 4	Newport Pagnell Town	1	Leighton Town	1	
Round 4	Tring Athletic	2	Walsall Wood	1	
Round 4	West Didsbury & Chorlton	2	Horden CW	0	
Round 5	AFC Wulfrunians	0	Congleton Town	1	
Round 5	Bridgwater United	0	Ascot United	1	
Round 5	Corsham Town	1	Brixham AFC	1	(aet)
	Corsham Town won 4-3 on penalties.				
Round 5	Coventry Sphinx	1	West Didsbury & Chorlton	1	(aet)
	West Didsbury & Chorlton won 3-1 on penalties.				
Round 5	Eccleshill United	0	Atherstone Town	2	
Round 5	Harefield United	0	Peacehaven & Telscombe	0	(aet)
	Peacehaven & Telscombe won 3-1 on penalties.				
Round 5	Newport Pagnell Town	1	Jersey Bulls	0	
Round 5	Tring Athletic	1	Bury AFC	2	
Round 6	Congleton Town	1	Bury AFC	1	(aet)
	Congleton Town won 5-4 on penalties.				
Round 6	Newport Pagnell Town	2	Atherstone Town	2	(aet)
	Newport Pagnell Town won 4-3 on penalties.				
Round 6	Peacehaven & Telscombe	1	Corsham Town	1	(aet)
	Corsham Town won 3-2 on penalties.				
Round 6	West Didsbury & Chorlton	1	Ascot United	1	(aet)
	Ascot United won 4-3 on penalties.				
Semi-final	Congleton Town	2	Newport Pagnell Town	2	(aet)
	Newport Pagnell Town won 3-2 on penalties.				
Semi-final	Corsham Town	2	Ascot United	2	(aet)
	Ascot United won 5-4 on penalties.				
FINAL	Ascot United	1	Newport Pagnell Town	0	